ORIENTALISMS OF THE HISPANIC AND LUSO-BRAZILIAN WORLD

EDITED BY
ARACELI TINAJERO

escribana
books

NEW YORK, 2014

Title: *Orientalisms of the Hispanic and Luso-Brazilian World*
ISBN-10: 1940075092
ISBN-13: 978-1-940075-09-9

Design: © Ana Paola González
Cover Disign: © Jhon Aguasaco
Cover Image: Sin título / Untitled (Shunga IV), 2007 © Dr. Lakra
Ink and acrylic on Japanese print (ukiyo-e)
24.5 x 16.6 cm (9.65 x 6.54 inches)
Courtesy of the artist and kurimanzutto, Mexico City
Photograph by: Michel Zabé & Omar Luis Olguin
Editor in Chief: Carlos Aguasaco
E-mail: carlos@artepoetica.com / aguasaco@gmail.com
Mail: 38-38 215 Place, Bayside, NY 11361, USA.

© *Orientalisms of the Hispanic and Luso-Brazilian World*, Araceli Tinajero
© *Orientalisms of the Hispanic and Luso-Brazilian World*, 2014 for this edition Escribana Books
an Imprint of Artepoética Press Inc.

Library of Congress subject headings:
Orientalism in literature — Latin America
Orientalism in art — Latin America
Orientalism — Latin America
Latin American literature — 20th century — History and criticism
Latin American literature — Asian influences
Spanish literature — 20th century — History and criticism
Spanish literature — Asian influences
Brazilian literature — 20th century — History and criticism
Brazilian literature — Asian influences
Portuguese literature — 20th century — History and criticism
Portuguese literature — Asian influences
Orient — In literature
Asia — In literature
Exoticism in literature — Latin America
Includes bibliographical references and index

To Dr. María Natividad López Tinajero
For her generosity and wisdom

TABLE OF CONTENTS

Acknowledgments

My fundamental thanks go to the Ph.D. Program of Hispanic and Luso-Brazilian Literatures of The Graduate Center (City University of New York), where I have taught, learned, and thrived since the fall of 2009. I thank José del Valle, Director of the Program, for giving me the opportunity to teach specialized doctoral seminars. It is always a delight to be able to teach and discuss topics with Ph.D. students.

Orientalism is a topic that I have explored for several years and thanks to the company, the example and the provocations of fellow scholars that share the same passions about the subject I have been able to learn so much. I must thank Gerard Aching, Aurelio Asiain, Nicholas Birns, Ricardo de la Fuente Ballesteros, Sonia Betancort Santos, Kenya C. Dowrkin y Méndez, Enrique Dussel Peters, Paulo Franchetti, Axel Gasquet, Koichi Hagimoto, Adrian Hearn, Evelyn Hu-Dehart, Takahiro Kato, James Krippner, Julia Kushigian, Kathleen López, Ignacio López-Calvo, Shigeko Mato, Seiko Ota, Cristián Ricci, Zelideth Maria Rivas, Jorge Ruedas de la Serna, for their support and the enriching ongoing dialogue about East-West encounters.

I would like to thank my friends with whom more often than not I maintain a fruitful intellectual dialogue. I sincerely thank Rolena Adorno, Álvaro Enrigue, K. David Jackson, Gilbert M. Joseph, Martin Lienhard, William Luis, Aníbal González Pérez, Carlos Alberto González Sánchez, Roberto González Echevarría, Floyd Merrell, Julio Ortega, Gustavo Pérez Firmat, Antonio José Ponte, Julio Ramos, Mónica Ricketts, Stefan Rinke, Rafael Rojas, Daniel Shapiro, Elzbieta Sklodowska, Doris Sommer, and Noël Valis. Thank you all for your generosity.

My colleagues and students at the City College of New York and The Graduate Center (City University of New York) are always very supportive. No list of dozens, even hundreds of people who play a very important role in shaping the inspiration for the concepts of my publications could even begin to do the matter of justice. I thank you all for your extraordinary company and insights.

I am very lucky to have exceptional librarians at the Cohen Library (The City College of New York). Daisy V. Domínguez and Yoko Inagi are truly exceptional. Thank you ever so much for your patience and support.

The distinguished scholar, Mauricio Font, director of the Bildner Center for Western Hemisphere Studies (where I am a fellow) has been very supportive for over a decade. His extraordinary enthusiasm and vision have made possible several interdisciplinary panels of discussion on the relationship between Latin America and Asia. Of course, all these events are possible thanks to the impeccable organization of our research assistants. My special thanks to Jonathan Aguirre and Rosalina López.

I would like to thank my dear colleague, I-Hsien Wu, for having convinced me to include Dr. Lakra's art piece in this book. He is an artist who I would love to hate but he is brilliant and exceptional. This is why I don't get tired of talking about his work everywhere I go.

The authors of this volume have been such a significant help in the preparation of this book that I can hardly say that I have edited it by my own. They all provided invaluable help at the different stages of preparing the manuscript. I thank you all for your commitment, your wonderful team-work spirit, your contribution and your patience.

Hugs and kisses to everyone in my family. You've always given me so much strength that I will not be able to thank you in one hundred years.

My most sincere thanks go out to Dr. Carlos Aguasaco of Artepoética Press for his professionalism and for his faith in this manuscript.

Introduction

It is almost impossible to understand any aspect of Orientalism without alluding to the classic book *Orientalism* (1978) by Edward Said. For the critic, "Orientalism" is a specific and complex phenomenon that explores representations of the Orient fabricated by Western cultures. Therefore, the act of "orientalizing" was a European invention (Said's study particularly deals with English and French discourses) based on the representation of exotic beings, romances, memories, evocative landscapes and extraordinary experiences. According to Said's theory, the European discourse about the Orient is based upon a relationship of power and domination that establishes an order of hierarchy and hegemony. The binary oppositions that are presented in his groundbreaking study are intimately related to the concepts of "center" and "periphery". Obviously it can be noted that the ideas of "center" and "periphery" have to do with a stance that is relative, psychological and ideologically rooted in European imperialism. With this in mind, how is it possible to study orientalist discourses produced by societies where there is no colony-empire relationship but rather relationships between post-colonial subjects? How do the representations that are not part of a hierarchical order manifest themselves, particularly in cases where there is no dichotomy between the conventions that have come to be known as the "center" and the "periphery"? Without any doubt, the complex interactions manifested in a "peripheral" discourse about another "periphery" offer alternatives that differentiate the order that is rooted in the "center-periphery" concept. In other words, it is not about inaugurating a stable and symmetrical system where the possibility of questioning discursive strategies and basic controversies does not exist when in fact they arise from an epistemological rupture. The same happens in the case of Spain's relationship with the Middle East. As it is known, the Iberian Peninsula was dominated by the Arabs for just over seven centuries.

Therefore, "Orientalism" from the Spanish view offers very different alternatives that should be studied taking into consideration their unique historical context.

The latest studies about Orientalisms of the Hispanic and Luso-Brazilian World offer a wide range of perspectives that enrich the field of Orientalist studies above all because they offer alternatives to the very phenomenon that Said judges. The important book by Julia Kushigian, *Orientalism in the Hispanic Literary Tradition: In Dialogue with Borges, Paz and Sarduy* was a significant pioneer study because in her introduction she discusses the importance of the Arabic heritage in the literary and cultural history of Spain. And in my book *Orientalismo en el modernismo hispanoamericano* I argue that all studies about the relationships between Latin America and the Far East should take into account the historic relationship and cultural exchange that existed for centuries between these two entities. Now that we are in the twenty-first century, globalization has provoked new publications both historical and artistic in nature; literature and criticism that invites us to continue studying these discourses in relation to the Middle East and the Far East from diverse points of view. At the same time, some studies are focusing on the reevaluation of classic texts. These new readings are very stimulating because they force us not only to re-read the texts but they also invite us to rethink the canon from different points of view.

The most recent historical studies that have been published focus on Asian communities in Brazil as well as in Peru, for example, *Encounters: People of Asian Descent in the Americas* by Rishni Rostmji-Kerns; *Herederos del dragón: Historia de la comunidad china en el Perú* by Humberto Rodríguez Pastor; *The Japanese in Latin America* by Daniel M. Masterson; *Mass Migration to Modern Latin America* edited by Samuel L. Baily and Eduardo José Míguez; as well as the most recent book by Matt K. Matsuda which covers other dimensions: *Pacific Worlds – A History of Seas, Peoples and Cultures*. There are some very interesting studies about the Chinese in Cuba such as *The Coolie Speaks*: *Chinese Indentured Laborers and African Slaves in Cuba* by Lisa Yun, and *Chinese Cubans: A Transnational History* by Kathleen López. *Siete migraciones japonesas en México*

1890-1978 by María Elena Ota Mishima and *Historia mínima de Japón edited by Michiko Tanaka* are key studies for understanding Japanese migration in Mexico; moreover, *The Chinese in Mexico 1882-1940* by Robert Chao Romero, and *Chinese Mexicans: Transpacific Migration and the Search for a Homeland 1910-1960* by Julia María Schiavone Camacho are valuable studies that help us understand the Asian presence in Mexico.

In the field of the arts there are various artists that deserve to be studied further. In other words, the work of Cuban Wifredo Lam has been widely studied but there are other contemporary Caribbean artist that deserve more attention such as in the case of Flora Fong from Cuba; Nicolás Dumit Estévez from the Dominican Republic; Tam Joseph from Dominica; and Elba Damast of Venezuela. Also, there are other Asian-Caribbean artists who do not come from Spanish-speaking countries but their art is eclectic and very original; for example in the case of Richard Fung, Carlisle Chang, Nicole Awai, Asha Ganpat, and Roshini Kempadoo from Trinidad or by Albert Chong and Lyn-Kee-Chow from Jamaica.

Mexico has very interesting artists that paint or produce Asian-themed pieces and here I am not referring exclusively to Pablo Vargas Lugo, Fernanda Brunet, Rodrigo Aldana or Edgar Orlaineta but also to others such as Luis Nishikawa, Kishio Murata or Shinzaburo Takeda (he was born in Japan but is Mexican by naturalization). In fact, the art of Dr. Lakra (the cover of this book bears an image created by him) is also incredibly daring and provocative. Only he would think of tattooing the faces, arms, and legs of a couple making love in a Japanese print (ukiyo-e). But the surprising thing is that in the painting the man is the one with the fewest tattoos because one of his arms is not tattooed at all. His work reminds us of the poem by José Juan Tablada, "La mujer tatuada." But not only do Mexican artists evoke Japan or any other place in Asia; the work of Urugayan Roberto Fernández Ibáñez exceptionally combines haiku with photography. And, the great artist Tomie Ohtake (Japanese but now Brazilian by naturalization) through her paintings and sculptures combines the space and organic aesthetics of Japanese art with Brazilian artistic traditions. In fact there are so many Brazilian artists of

11

Japanese descent that a study of their work would fill at least three volumes. This is only a list of contemporary artists: http://www.imigrantesjaponeses.com.br/PintoresConteporaneos.pdf

The literature of the Hispanic and Luso-Brazilian World that focuses on Asian cultures has proliferated as well. The following are some examples of the narrative titles that have been published during the last two decades: *Teoría del alma china* by Carlos Aguilera; *Sho-shan y la dama oscura* as well as *Tinta violeta* by Eve Gil; *Gaijin* by Maximiliano Matayoshi; *El jardín japonés* by Antonio Ortuño; *Cuentos completos* by Siu Kam Wen; *Una novela china* by César Aira; *El ombligo del dragón* by Ximena Sánchez Echenique; *Un chino en bicicleta* byAriel Magnus; *Lunas de miel* by Luisa Futoransky; *La eternidad del instante* by Zoé Valdés; *La cola de la serpiente* by Leonardo Padura; *Aprendices de brujo* by Antonio Orlando Rodríguez; *Los impostores* by Santiago Gamboa; *Cartas de Tepoztlán* and *El misterio de los tigres* by Pablo Soler Frost; *La profundidad de la piel* by Pedro Ángel Palou; *Trenes hacia Tokio* and *Tatami* by Alberto Olmos; *China para hipocondríacos* and *Mujeres que viajan solas* by José Ovejero; *Japón* by Lolita Bosch and Alberto Olmos; *Caminos para la paz: literatura israelí y árabe en castellano*, edited by Ignacio López Calvo y Cristián H. Ricci; *A descoberta da América pelos turcos* by Jorge Amado; *Vozes no deserto* by Nélida Piñón; *Rakushisha* by Adriana Lisboa; *Um estranho em Goa* by José Eduardo Agualusa; *Jerusalem* by Gonçalo M. Tavares, etcetera. The re-readings of literature written in Portuguese are very interesting, for example, *O Japão* by Aluísio de Azevedo; *O mandarin* by Eça de Queirós; the poetry of Fernando Pessoa, Wenceslau de Moraes and António Manuel Couto and the chronicles of the sixteenth century written by Fernão Lopes de Castanheda, João de Barros and Gaspar Correia. These are only a few examples.

Without a doubt, the emerging literary criticism on Orientalism reflects the themes and preoccupations from the latest literary creations as well as from the re-reading of some texts that deserve to be studied in the light of a new perspective. For example, the editions by Ignacio López-Calvo, *Alternative Orientalisms in Latin America and Beyond*; *One Periphery Reads the Other: Knowing the "Oriental" in the Americas and Ibe-*

rian Peninsula; and *Peripheral Transmodernities: South-to-South Intercultural Dialogues between the Luso-Hispanic World and "the Orient"* present a series of articles that explore the diverse possibilities of studying Orientalism particularly by means of both historical and contemporary literature. The same applies to the interdisciplinary volume edited by Erik Camayd-Freixas, *Orientalism and Identity in Latin America. Fashioning Self and Other from the (Post) Colonial Margin*. Other studies have focused on writers of Asian descent in Peru such as *Three Asian Hispanic Writers from Peru: Doris Moromisato, José Watanabe and Siu Kam Wen* by Debbie Lee-DiStefano and *The Closed Hand. Images of the Japanese in Modern Peruvian Literature* by Rebecca Riger Tsurumi. In the case of Argentina, *Oriente al sur: el orientalismo literario argentino* de *Esteban Echeverría a Roberto Arlt* by Axel Gasquet, and the doctoral thesis "Oriente no es una pieza de museo: Jorge Luis Borges y las culturas de la India" by Sonia Betancort Santos-are exceptional works. The book *Disorientations: Spanish Colonialism in Africa and the Performance of Identity* by Susan Martin-Márquez and *The Return of the Moor: Spanish Responses to Contemporary Moroccan Immigration* by Daniela Flesler teach us to reevaluate the historical and contemporary relationships between the Iberian Peninsula and the Arab world. The historical and literary relationships between the last Spanish colonies are also being studied, for example in the book by Koichi Hagimoto, *Between Empires: Martí, Rizal and the Intercolonial Alliance*. The editions *ArabAmericas: Literary Entanglements of the American Hemisphere and the Arab World*, edited by Ottmar Ette and Friederike Pannewick; *Asia and the Asians in the Contemporary Spanish Imaginary* edited by Yeon-Soo Kim; *Moros en la costa: orientalismo en Latinoamérica*, edited by Silvia Nagy-Zekmi; *Orientalismos: oriente y occidente en la literatura y las artes de España e Hispanoamerica*, edited by Joan Torres-Pou; as well as the special numbers in the journals *Review: Literature and Arts of the Americas* (72, Vol. 39, 2006); *Siglo Diecinueve (Literatura Hispánica)* No. 17 (2011); *Studi Ispanici* (XXXIII, 2008); and all the issues of *TRANSMODERNITY: Journal of Peripheral Cultural Production of the Luso-Hispanic World* offer dozens of very serious and stimulating articles. Also, four important editions that offer groundbreaking research dealing with the history, culture and literature of the Portuguese-speaking world should be recognized: *Fiction in the Portuguese-Speaking World* edited by Charles M. Kelley; *The Post-Colonial Literature of Lusophone Africa* edited by Patrick Chabal; *Portuguese and Luso-Asian Legacies in Southeast Asia, 1511-2011* and *Culture and Identity in the Luso-Asian World: Tenacities & Plasticities*, edited by Laura Jarnagin; as well as *Lusofonia: Encruzilhadas Culturais*, edited by Ana Maria Corriea and Ivo Carneiro de Sousa. Finally I would like to mention one essential book that studies the literature written in Spanish: *The Magellan Fallacy. Globalization and the Emergence of Asian and African Literature in Spanish* by Adam Lifshey.

The most recent critical studies reflect the themes of the emerging literature or new approaches to reading the classical texts mentioned above. These focus on race and ethnicity, Asian and Middle-Eastern immigration in Spain and Latin America, tourism, Asian aesthetics and artifacts, Asian cultural consumption in Hispanic cultures, the process of assimilation within the Asian communities that emigrated to Europe or Latin America, how the Asian continent presents itself in the view of Latin American travelers, the way in which the oriental subject represents itself in art and literature; what kind of relationship exists between Asian communities and other minority groups in a specific country; what are the assimilation policies, the representation of Asian women and Arabs both in eastern texts as well is in western ones, transnationalism and exile of Asians and Arabs; the list is infinite.

As we have seen above, during the last two decades several books on the Western-Eastern encounters have been published. With the exception of two chapters, *Orientalisms of the Hispanic and Luso-Brazilian World* studies some of the most recent fiction (short stories, novels, and poems) and non-fiction (essays and chronicles) written in the Hispanic and Luso-Brazilian world. This volume not only offers a new approach to the way we look at and study current writers of Spanish and Portuguese expression but it also deepens our understanding of Orientalism.

In the first chapter Paulo Franchetti offers a comparative study of the sense of exile and the initial shock of the different—the exotic—in two Portuguese writers: Camilo Pessanha and Wenceslau de Moraes. The first, although his book was published fairly recently in 1920 and his verses circulated in manuscripts and other loose publications, is now considered among the great poets of the Portuguese language and has exercised a profound influence on literary modernists. The second was, for many years, the primary chronicler of the Orient in the Portuguese language, writing for many newspapers and regularly publishing books on the subjects of China and Japan. Franchetti suggests that both of these writers are pivotal in the renewal of Portuguese literary thought.

Among the many interpolated stories in João Guimarães Rosa's masterpiece, *Grande sertão: veredas* (1956), the case of Maria Mutema has attracted a great deal of critical scholarship due to its thematic content. According to traditional criticism, Maria Mutema's case deals with the question of the existence of Absolute Evil. In chapter two, Jizelda Galvão suggests a hermeneutic shift in the perspective of the Mutema case. Rosa's main reason for interpolating this case lies in its theme of enlightenment. He signals his intentions for the story through the name "Mutema," where the key term "Mu" from Zen Buddhism is added to the Portuguese word for "theme" (tema). "Mu" literally means emptiness, nothingness, in Japanese, so the story of Mutema introduces the theme of emptiness, that is, enlightenment, into the novel. The Mutema case is introduced as a *koan*, a Zen-Buddhist narrative practice used by monks to reach enlightenment through meditation on a question or a story. The language utilized by Rosa to narrate *Grande sertão: veredas* shares several characteristics (which the author discusses in this chapter) with the koan. By incorporating the theme of enlightenment into his larger narrative, Galvão emphasizes that Rosa not only builds a thematic inter-textual bridge to the Orient, but a linguistic one as well.

Chapter three makes a shift from the Latin American gaze and takes us to Europe. As of late there has been a certain media interest in rediscovering one particular time period within Spanish history: the former Spanish Protectorate that existed from 1913 to 1958. However, this relatively short period in Spain's history is contextualized by the fact that the country has occupied a unique position amongst the former empires of Europe. No other colonial power similar to Spain had itself been colonized; however, the Iberian Peninsula was, for almost eight hundred years, a colonial possession and caliphate of the Arab empire. In this chapter Christina Vázquez Mauricio analyzes the development of various strains of Orientalism throughout the pages of one such resurgence of interest in Spanish Morocco: María Dueñas' *El tiempo entre costuras* (2009), a novel that examines the Spanish-Arab relationship in the 1930s and 40s. In her analysis Vázquez Mauricio pays particular attention to the vision of Morocco in Spain, to the vision of Spain in Morocco, and how tangible elements such as clothing and cultural artifacts are employed to illustrate Orientalism in a Spanish-Arab perspective.

In chapter four Kenneth Yanes offers a unique study focusing chiefly on a collection of short stories by Mohamed Akalay, *Entre Tánger y Larache* (2006), which depicts the tensions that exist today within the hybrid language and space of a "peripheral Moroccan culture" embedded in the West. Akalay's work presents his audience with a dialogue that thrives between the Orient and the Occident in which a Moroccan appropriates the Castilian language and this act does not come without its complications. Akalay's collection of short stories presents a conflict of style between Moroccan *costumbrista* literature – didactic and moralizing with its roots in Arabic oral traditions – and Western literature with an esthetic tradition rooted in elements of metaphor, symbolism, allusions and Orientalism. Akalay's readers (and the characters in his works) are dispersed on both sides of the Strait of Gibraltar. Moroccan writers of Castilian expression maintain the *costumbrista* tradition for their Moroccan readers, which are filled with moralizing fables, proverbs from the Quran and realism of the daily life of a Moroccan that for many has lead to the decision of leaving the country to find a better life in the West. While writing to a Spanish or Western audience, these writers aim to incorporate literary esthetics with the *costumbrista* tradition; it is here where one finds the occidentalization of Moroccan literature. Through the act of writing in Castilian, a language bequeathed to a select few in the north of Morocco during the time of colonization, writers such as Akalay begin to occidentalize their writing, which is further developed through the use of Western literary style. They are adopting a language of the occidental "Other" in order to be understood, but, in order to be understood and remain engaging, writers such as Akalay also run the risk of self-orientalizing.

In chapter five Kathryn Mendez analyzes four novels by Mario Bellatín; two older novels (*El jardín de la señora Murakami* [2000] and *Shiki Nagaoka: una nariz de ficción* [2001]) in comparison with two of his more recent novels (*La clase muerta* [2011] and *Disecado* [2011]) as being works that explore the human body, its relationship with the presence of ghostly figures and both internal and external spaces. Bellatín constantly tries to walk along the blurred lines between autobiography, perceived reality, and fiction. In this chapter Mendez argues that the use of photography, autobiographical references, footnotes and appendixes is part of a project that Bellatín creates to purposefully make his fiction appear to be reality. His work is closely related to some of the Latin American Orientalist works of Rubén Darío and Jorge Luis Borges, two authors who are also known to use imagery of nature and death simultaneously. Mendez emphasizes that the presence of interior and exterior spaces, gardens and nature is very important to these works, particularly in the way that they are connected to the protagonists' physical and mental states.

Lastly, in chapter six Jennifer Prince analyzes the 2011 novel *Verde Shanghai*. Written by Mexican author Cristina Rivera Garza, the novel tells the complex story of Marina, a young married woman, in search of a being that haunts her: another young woman named Xian. This search leads Marina into the *barrio chino* of Mexico City, a place where she can leave behind her husband and married life and begin to discover her real identity. Prince explores how the complex relationships of Orientalism help to define Marina, specifically using the theory of Edward Said and Julia Kushigian, along with ways in which identity can be established through these relationships of Subject and Other. With a focus especially on the possible connection between Marina and the mysterious

Xian, the author examines the convergence of the Subject and the Other. Yet the author also emphasizes that the works of Argentine author Jorge Luis Borges—through his short stories with Oriental themes that have much in common with *Verde Shanghai*—since he provides possible solutions to the many questions of identity that the novel creates

Orientalisms of the Hispanic and Luso-Brazilian World is an important book because it offers innovative perspectives that help us better understand the relationship between East and West. Without any doubt, the themes and analyses presented here by means of recently published literary texts as well as re-readings of classics will open new avenues of research that will continue to enrich the field of Orientalist studies.

Part one:

Luso-brazilian orientalisms

Camilo Pessanha and Wenceslau de Moraes: Images from China and Japan

Paulo Franchetti

In the transition from the nineteenth century to the twentieth, two Portuguese writers became well-known for making the exile experience the core of their work or public image: Wenceslau de Moraes and Camilo Pessanha.

Both lived in Macao in 1894 as teachers of the newly-created school *Liceu de Macao*. After this, Moraes moved to Japan, where he held the post of consul of his country in Kobe. After finally stepping down as consul, he moved to the small provincial town of Tokushima where he continued to send to Portugal his reports on Japanese life and his reflections on the country. It was through Wenceslau de Moraes that generations of Portuguese readers came to know the art, literature and customs of Japan.

Camilo Pessanha settled in Macao, where besides teaching, he practiced law and became a member of the judiciary. Being the suspect of *"achinesamento"*[1] for having lived with a Chinese woman (with whom he had a son), for smoking opium, and for painstakingly and passionately devoting himself to the study of language and Chinese art, a baseless, enigmatic image was created of him that has since been dismantled.[2] Considered one of the great Portuguese poets, Pessanha was also a great collector of Chinese art and objects, having donated to the Portuguese state the result of his many years of research and work. Unfortunately, this

---

1 Having an affinity for the Chinese way of life and ideas, and adopting certain Chinese customs.
2 Franchetti, Paulo. *Camilo Pessanha*. Lisboa: Impresa Nacional/Casa da Moeda, 2008.

collection was poorly treated in its country and hitherto not appreciated.[3]

For Moraes and for Pessanha, exile, above all else, was the means through which Western artistic sensibility attempted to understand the different. Reflecting on the difference and, especially, on the difference in regards to art and its relationship with everyday life, constitutes the what is most noteworthy in their writings about the countries where they had chosen to live and die.

This article proceeds with a brief comparative study of the sense of exile through contact with the exotic in these two important Portuguese authors.

1. The exoticism of Wenceslau de Moraes

In a chapter of *O-Yoné and Ko-Haru* (Imprensa Nacional/Casa da Moeda, 2006), entitled "The Japanese exoticism", Wenceslau de Moraes tells the impetus for the trip and for settling on the diverse, that characterizes his life and his work:

> One of the many interesting manifestations of the psychology of the European is undoubtedly love, felt by many individuals, for foreign and distant countries, for exotic civilizations.
> [...]
> When I speak of lovers of exoticism, I refer only to a small group of men, those who give everything for the exotic, those that in the name of exoticism lose all and become enslaved to it, those who are attracted by the strange and towards the strange are headed; fleeing, if they can, to their environment,

---

3 A neglect and abjection history: this is how one could characterize the treatment that the Portuguese government gave the rich collection that has been donated by one of Portugal's greatest poets. Other than the prejudice against the "*achinesado*," nothing else can explain the continued scandal. Currently, a part of the Camilo Pessanha collection is finally exhibited in the Orient Museum, in Lisbon, but in a chaotic way, paying no mind to the preservation of the collection's unity.

trying to identify themselves as much as possible with the new environment, resolutely divorced from society, so different, from where they were born. (Moraes 2006, 133)

The sequence of the text shows that Moraes believes that exoticism is a substitute for religious fervor—that is, the radical perception of difference and displacement, and the longing for an ideal of perfection:

> Some more sensitive people, who should be, if they had come into this world a few centuries ago, fervent supporters of the church of the popes, hieratic inhabitants of monasteries and wilderness, today are mere mystical aesthetes; and, among the hypocrisy, selfishness, and general indifference of the time, the came the advent of a religion that substitutes another religion within the restricted circle of certain ideal worshipers. Thus, it can be said that, categorically, nowadays Europe is the most unfit means for the worship of the aesthetic, pure and naïve. (Moraes, 2006, 134)

The displacement in space, therefore, is also an anachronistic path. An *arebours* movement. To move to the "far away" is also moving to the "back there," it is not only to escape from the civilization itself, but also from his present time. And as Western civilization—this vector for a future sense is always worse from the aesthetic point of view—also scatters through space, the search for the exotic places not only the removal from Western culture at the center, but also at the margins, and it is increasingly difficult to find culturally preserved spaces: "However, beauty and art still exist, far away, quite far away, although the Western invasion, yore religious and today mercantile, domineering and always oppressive, is careful by all means to destroy them, denaturalizing and denationalizing populations" (Moraes 2006, 135).

Thus, Moraes is the man who seeks in the East what he no longer believes he can find in the West: basically, a daily life marked by kindness and a sense for the beautiful, by the integration of everyday activities in a line of continuity with the past that enriches and ennobles them.

This is why his movement in space is not a gluttonous seeking of sensations. What is new does not matter to this kind of exoticism, but what is strange. Moraes does not belong to the class of tourist that seeks what is picturesque, only later to return to the safety of his place of origin. He is rather an aesthete, who seeks the strange as an antidote for and a critique of weakening sensations, produced by modernity.

What makes Moraes' exoticism painful is the understanding that the stranger – that is, the experience of diversity – continuously disappears, barely surviving – and who knows for how long – in the farthest of distances, since the modern, homogenizing west gradually invades every corner of the earth.

His own journey is a model of this "getaway from the West": to Africa, then to coastal China, to cities in Japan, and finally—when Japan is westernized in administrative or port cities—to a forgotten village in the countryside.

The exotic removal, while allowing the possibility of finding afar what is missing at the place of origin, is also a way of producing the past of the origin. To freeze something in time that, at the very origin, one feels to be deteriorating. Hence, the voyage without return appears in his work as a way to stop the flow of time, maintaining and depurating, in memory, his homeland affections.

Through the emotional recovery of the essence of what was left voluntarily before its major degradation, what was lost is ideally reconstructed from the conquered. Feeling that his home country was marching towards collapse, once he begins living in Japan he also begins to idolize Portugal; therefore, in relation to the origin and destination, the basic attitude that organizes his text is a sense of longing. A longing is never confused with nostalgia, with desire or the hope of return. This is the intimate form of his exoticism; the painful evocations from the first enchantments with Japan are repeated in each book, and especially, his defunct loves in the Land of the Rising Sun. In his work, the "religion of the ideal" is transmuted into "religion of the longing", which gives the specific *pathos* of his more pungent books, which are the *Bon-odori in Tokushima* and *O-Yoné and Ko-Haru*.

What Moraes searches for in the past is not a harbinger for the present or its cause, but that which did not have continuity, or irretrievably was lost. His literature is nourished by and flourishes with full awareness of loss and impossibility of integration or reintegration.

With the affirmation of the diverse and the coexistence of what is irreconcilable is founded what could be called the ethics of his works: tolerance, acceptance of difference, and humility. In this case, it would not be an exaggeration to say that the exoticism of Moraes is a type of ascent – at least in the Buddhist manner, considering that his Japanese life in Tokushima was guided by the ideals of divestment, simplicity and compassion for living beings.

Without being Buddhist or Shintoist, it is certain that Moraes, as appears in *O-Yoné and Ko-Haru* and in *The Bon-odori in Tokushima*, is a hermit, engaged in the practice of the cardinal virtues of the art of *haikai* that he so much appreciated: *sabi*, *wabi* and *karumi*. That is, a type of combination of delight in the experience of solitude, in contemplation of impermanence and poverty exercise with the minimum necessary complaisance and simplicity of disconnected expression.

2. The exoticism according to Camilo Pessanha

For him, the displacement in space is not won or pursuit of the ideal. Rather, it is emptying, loss of substance: "And I, who had missed when I was leaving, even Barcelona, where I had been for five days, to Colombo where I had been for two hours. Because we are a small drop of blood, undoing ourselves and staying everywhere" (Pessanha 1984, 47).

It is the feeling derived from this perception of loss of substance that the poet generically calls "saudade" (nostalgia). But his longing has a special color: less than a perspective of emotive recovery of something that was lost, it is a feeling that is defined by the irreversible consciousness lost and the consequences of this perception, wherever there be the weakening and the gradual increasing of pain caused by separation.

His aesthetic is based on seeking to express, to pin down the inner feelings and emotions experienced by the subject that has been pulled out of his/her environment. His own memory, seen through the metaphor of the small drop of blood, is thus reduced to a kind of painful consciousness of the inevitable decline of vital energy.

Therefore, Pessanha at first is not going to find anything but horror in the place he calls exile. Macao becomes a meeting point for all degenerations. "A mess," he says, and adds: "material and moral."

But it is not only Macao that seems to be disagreeable, but also China as a whole, an object of an intense feeling of disgust and aversion. The way he connects himself with the strange is like a scientist or an archaeologist, dedicated to the analysis of a monstrous object.

He arrived in Macao in 1894; 16 years later he was still writing about China: "A deformed civilization, in which can be seen, even in periods of greatest splendor, the scar of the most distant barbarism" (Pires 1992, 115-116).

And in a text written between 1910 and 1912 (published just in 1912), the Middle Kingdom seemed to him a jungle of physical and moral diseases that he is delighted to describe:

> The deformity, monstrosity, rickets, dwarfism, cretinism.... Tuberculosis, syphilis, hysteria, epilepsy, chorea, leprosy, scabies.... The prostitution, debauchery, pederasty, sadism.... Fraud, extortion, theft, robbery, banditry, piracy, captivity.... And all this every day, ... trash heap composed of the most disgusting wastes, sewage flow dragging the most recognizable human dross. Ignorance, coarseness, superstition, disloyalty, cowardice, avarice, lust, cruelty, impudence, cynicism, moral lethargy.... (Pires 1992, 124)

Meanwhile, soon thereafter in the same text, this circus of horrors turns into a great compliment of China, its art and its code of justice, of which he writes: "As for an interpretation from a legal point of view, of human actions, it is, through the accuracy of observation that is demonstrated and by the high spirit of justice and goodness that inspires it, one of the most astonishing monuments to wisdom bequeathed by the centuries" (Pires 1992, 149).

The change is not explained as a discursive strategy. The division of the text into two opposing parts marks a turning point in the way Pessanha perceives and relates to China. A turning point that might also be explained by the revolution that shook the former imperial country, paving the way for the China we know today.

Be what it may, the initial aversion to the West shown in this text was overcome and the qualities of Chinese character were understood-the main quality being the aversion to the West and the rejection of its homogenizing power:

> Systematic resistance, natural and invincible, to the invasion of the industrial cosmopolite, without any foreign innovation attempting to adapt, transforming it, to its peculiar ethnic physiognomy and to the global harmony of its civilization, in order to keep this, in the minute details of its manifestations, an accurate character of originality, so different from that exoticism, indigent and bastard, of all other non-Christian countries, for the use of globe-trotters and undemanding in its curiosity, – the resistance of inert antipathy, more effective than the "great wall", than that solidary crowd that instinctively opposes any Western influence. (Pires 1992, 151)

In this observation, Pessanha speaks like Moraes, but never refers to China with that immediate affectionate integration that Moraes will have regarding Japan.

On the contrary, the metaphor of his relationship with China is the experience that Carlos Amaro narrates, in a letter dated 1909, written shortly after leaving Singapore:

Among these fruits there was one I especially had great desire to know, – the durian. It is celebrated for its delicious taste and its awful smell. It is said that whoever became accustomed to it loves it like an addiction, irresistibly. Indeed, it must be as such; so complex is its flavor that after a while in the mouth, the palate will always go on discovering new delights. Its smell, strong when the fruit is open, surprises with a characteristic smell of latrine, but little by little its perfume is discovered, composed of many perfumes.... (Miguel, 137)

It is through the study of the language, art, law and traditional Chinese culture that Pessanha converts his initial repugnance in affection.

The word may seem exaggerated, as far as the assertion of a continuing intellectual activity of the poet. But I am sure they are accurate.

In fact, until now we knew little about Pessanha's dedication to the study of the things in China and none of the poet's personal documents after 1909 told us anything about how was the second half of his life in China.

Because of the enmity he created in Macao, his image became defined in the same vein as Camilo Pessanha over a long period of time: abulic, an opium addict, incapable of productivity since the early days of his arrival in Macao.

All was futile against this image: the dating of the poems written there, the publication of some Chinese translations in 1914, or the compilation of scattered texts by João de Castro Osório in the book *China*.

Until recently, only indirect testimony of Pessanha's dedication to Chinese studies where known, aside from his art collection, which today is finally open to the public. The most impressive is Carlos Amaro's testimony, who in 1926 claimed to have seen an enormous amount of translations and studies of Chinese literature and culture: "More than seven thousand pages [...] handwriting almost microscopic, from the last time Camilo Pessanha was in Lisbon" (Pires 1990, 75).

Today, however, there are a few new documents: the rest of the poet's letters to Carlos Amaro are finally being made public.

Its transcription here, first hand, is only possible thanks to the invaluable generosity of Daniel Pires who sent them to me as he was transcribing them.[4]

The first text is an excerpt from a letter dated March 8, 1912.

Here is what he writes to Carlos Amaro, asking the intercession of his friend to avoid him from being transferred elsewhere, outside of China:

> In almost twenty years in Macao, I have been adapting myself to the environment by means of a painful job, although partly unconsciously, it has incapacitated me to be anything anywhere but here! It has almost been twenty years since I began my more or less assiduous study of the Chinese language, Chinese customs, and Chinese art. The language, primarily since I was last here three years ago, I have been studying brutally—in furor to absorb myself in anything, to see if I could distract myself from the many miseries that I cannot change and that are my obsession.
>
> I have abandoned this study as of four months ago, temporarily because of my service as judge that does not leave me time for it. I was then engaged in completing the almost finished translation to prose of a great elegiac songbook from the Ming dynasty,—a unique and tiny piece that I would like to leave in print, or at least complete, as a memento of my gratitude to those who find a compassionate

---

4 When I drafted this chapter, the letters were clearly inedited. Given their importance, I recommended to Editora da Unicamp that they be published as a volume in a joint publication with Biblioteca Nacional de Portugal. The references to the page numbers proceed from that volume, which was launched in the beginning of 2013.

interest in the imperfections of my soul and the anguish of my life.

Moreover, of the little I earn, which has left me spending in daily essentials, I have used it in the acquisition of old furniture, —broken items and Chinese dolls-that I will probably never have enough money to move there, although upon my death it is my greatest wish that they remain stored in any of the national museums. To leave here on this way would be to renounce forever the possession of this poor collection that is almost the only solace of my eyes and my soul. Nothing is worth in money (at most a couple thousand *réis*, where some lawyers here, living an abundant life, have made a fortune in three years) – but, to gather this, it has cost me enormous sacrifices of every kind and it represents my savings and my work of almost my whole life.

Now all this—Chinese writings, Chinese poetry, Chinese art—how could they serve me anywhere but here? And what other new objects could occupy my spirit, in other lands, old, sick and despondent? (Pessanha 2012, 181)

Subsequently, on September 21st, 1912, he talks about the subject again:

As you know, I've been here almost twenty years and during that time I have exclusively applied the efforts of my intelligence to this exotic world.

[...] It is clear that my life needed an objective – otherwise I would die of sadness. And what other objective could I have here if not the study of the Chinese language, Chinese customs, Chinese art? The intellectual and moral loneliness in these environments is absolute. Here there is only a pitiful scum... I have, therefore, studied with furor up to what my scarce strengths allow.

I have learned to speak the Chinese language (I speak the Cantonese dialect fluently), and a little reading and writing. (Pessanha 2012, 186-187)

Pessanha, like Moraes, felt that the East was exile and "moral suicide" (the phrase is from the latter). But the legend that he had a vegetative life there is not true. On the contrary, he devoted himself to learning the language, culture and ancient civilization that he faced. [5]

And it is licit to imagine that if the documents he left in his office were not lost, the poet, in regards the dissemination of classical Chinese culture, would today be an equivalent of what Wenceslau de Moraes was for Japan.

Both have deepened in the contemplation and study of the exotic, but their paths are very diverse.

Moraes' Japanese work is a story of enchantment. He never ponders going back to Portugal. And he does not. Portugal, as is the Japan of *O-Yoné and Ko-Haru*—and like they themselves—ends up being a retrospective idealization, a spiritual building on the pain of dislocation and lack. An irreducible, unknowable object.

Yet the story of Pessanha, with respect to what he says about exoticism, is a conversion one that goes from horror to admiration and finally appreciation.

Pessanha's work can be described as an oscillation between two poles: nostalgia and melancholy. During the predominance of the first pole—that is, a general feeling of nostalgia—the writer constantly anguishes to return to Portugal. He even describes the poetic ability and his personal energy as dependent upon contact with his homeland.

But over time, unlike Moraes, not only does the nostalgia for his homeland depress him, but the negative idealization of the place of his origin takes over.

This is evidenced by this excerpt of another letter to Carlos Amaro, dated July 10th, 1916, written in Macao shortly after his return on what would be his last trip to Portugal:

---

5 Pessanha really had curious attitudes, which way does not match the abulic profile that the biographical fantasy was drawing about him, for example, the enthusiasm with which he participated, in 1911, of the foundation of a Shooting Association, dedicated to defending the territory of Macao. (I also owe this information to the researcher Daniel Pires, who recently discovered this curious fact.)

At least here, returned to my habits of spiritual solitude, nothing calls attention to my ulcerated soul, to exacerbate the sorrow. The environment is benign, because it is familiar to me: it is impregnated with myself, as I with him. It was a long and painful work of adaptation, but it is completed: now all of the disturbances of this equilibrium established overflow in suffering. I can count those five months of anxious agitation in which I struggled among the most horrible of my life. (Pessanha 2012, 193)

The sign is now reversed: staying in Portugal does not provide comfort but instead renews the feeling of inadequacy. Moreover, the movement of nostalgic idealization does not remain in Pessanha's text as it does in Moraes'. For the poet, Portugal comes to be a place of pain and anguish, to the point that he abruptly interrupts his last license, in 1916, eager to return to China. Not for lack of opium, as the legend would have us believe, but—paradoxically – because he now feels more integrated into the solitude of exile than that of his own motherland.

Hence the anguish with which he will express himself in 1924 at conference on Camões. Here, at the end of his life, he not only celebrates the memory of the poet that had disappeared five hundred years earlier, but also makes a confession of his own inability, while in exile, to keep alive the memento of the ideal homeland or to recover it through memory and longing.

The contact with his decadent and hostile home landing 1915-16 will constitute the poet's most deceptive experience. Redirected by it, his life and spiritual solitude in exile that led him to the study of Chinese, to the organization of an art collection and to translation, appear to him as something akin to happiness.

Hence, by different means and with different dynamics, Camilo Pessanha isolates himself in Macao and Moraes exiles himself in Tokushima. But while the latter entertains the West with a loose prose that tells of the infatuated experience with the different, Pessanha mutes himself, only speaking through the texts he studies, translates, and will eventually be lost, and flees from all that is representative of Europe. He does so to the point that he does not even occupy himself with *Clepsidra*, which will be published four years later and will only merit a late, distant, and formal memory.

BIBLIOGRAPHY

Franchetti, Paulo. *Camilo Pessanha*. Lisboa: Impresa Nacional/Casa da Moeda, 2008.

Miguel, António Dias. *Camilo Pessanha – elementos para o estudo da sua vida e da sua obra*. Lisbon: Edição de Álvaro Pinto, n.d. Print.

Moraes, Wenceslau de. *O "Bon-odori" em Tokushima*. 2nd ed. Porto: Companhia Portuguesa Editora L^{da}, n.d. Print.

—. *Ó-Yoné e Ko-Haru*. Lisbon: Imprensa Nacional-Casa da Moeda/ Instituto Camões, 2006. Print.

Pessanha, Camilo. *Cartas a Alberto Osório de Castro, João Baptista de Castro e Ana de Castro Osório*. Lisbon: Imprensa Nacional-Casa da Moeda, 1984. Print.

—. *Correspondência, dedicatórias e outros textos*. Org., pref., cronologia e notas de Daniel Pires. Lisboa: Biblioteca Nacional de Portugal ; Campinas: Editora da Unicamp, 2012.

Pires, Daniel. *Camilo Pessanha prosador e tradutor*. Macau: Instituto Português do Oriente/Instituto Cultural de Macau, 1992. Print.

—. *Homenagem a Camilo Pessanha*. Macau: Instituto Português do Oriente/Instituto Cultural de Macau, 1990. Print.

The Mu-theme in *Grande sertão: veredas*

Jizelda F. Galvão

> *Mas, esse norteado, tem. Tem que ter. Se não,*
> *a vida de todos ficava sendo sempre o confuso dessa*
> *doideira que é.*
> Riobaldo[6]

A "neophyte," on opening *Grande sertão: veredas*[7] for the first time, will come upon an unusual beginning consisting of a single word: "Nonada" (3). The reader's first reaction is to presuppose that the word is one of Rosa's many verbal creations. Instead, it's an archaic form that Rosa rescued from the dictionary.[8] Much has been written on this intriguing beginning, as scholars attempt to figure out what Rosa really meant by that word – nonada – beyond its common meaning (nothing, a trifle). As with much of Rosa's writing, the word seems to point in several directions at once. Nei Leandro de Castro, for example, shows us that the meaning of "nonada" has been linked to existentialist philosophy by quoting Vilem Flusser's analysis of the word: "A negação do *nichts* heideggeriano e do *néant* sartriano é o ponto de partida do *Grande Sertão* com suas veredas" (Castro 110). In contrast, an interesting neoplatonist twist is given to the term by Heitor Martins:

---

6 From *Grande sertão: veredas*. "But this path exists. It must. If not, our lives would always be this chaotic madness that it is (692-93)." All the translations of citations from *Grande sertão: veredas* that appear in this chapter were done by me.

7 I will be referring to Rosa's novel by the abbreviation GSV throughout this article. The page numbers in parentheses refer to the novel GSV unless otherwise indicated.

8 Nonada. [De non, f. arcaica de 'não', + ada.] s.f.v. ninharia (Ferreira 1198).

> [S]eria demasiado sugerir que este nonada é ain-
> da uma homenagem a Plotino? [...] uma 'tradução'
> popular do próprio título da obra de Plotino, Enéa-
> das, que quer dizer séries de nove, na linguagem
> sertaneja de nonada. *Grande Sertão: Veredas* seria
> então uma enéada de Guimarães Rosa, semicamu-
> flada com buritis e capim, uma nonada que trata
> do problema da habitação do Mal no mundo, na
> constante ronda de seu redemoinho, [...]. (92)

According to Rafael Bluteau, the word "nonada" is composed of two negations: "não ou no" and "nada" (Bluteau 745).
Therefore, I will argue that Rosa is being very faithful to the
archaic concept carried within the root of the word – nothingness. Furthermore, with "nonada," Rosa is building an
inter-textual bridge between his novel and an ancient Asian
narrative style – the koan.

The "koan is the Japanese pronunciation of the Chinese
characters *kung an*, which mean 'public record'" states John F.
Fisher. And he adds that these characters were used by Bud-
dhists to signify "a public document setting up a standard of
judgment [...]" (65). According to Isshu Miura:

> When [master Chung-fêng Ming-pên] was
> asked why the teachings of the buddhas and pa-
> triarchs were called 'public records', that is, koans,
> he replied: The koans may be compared to the case
> records of the public law court. Whether or not the
> ruler succeeds in bringing order to his realm de-
> pends in essence upon the existence of law. Kung
> (ko), or 'public', is *the single track* followed by all
> sages and worthy men alike, *the highest principle
> which serves as a road for the whole world*. And (an), or
> 'records", are the orthodox writings which record
> what the sages and worthy men regard as princi-
> ples. (4-5, my emphases)

Rosa's familiarity with Oriental philosophy is very well
documented. Francis Utéza, in his book, *João Guimarães Rosa:*

Metafísica do Grande Sertão, presents an extensive commentary on Rosa's library (32 – 39) in which he lists quite a few titles owned by Rosa concerning Asian traditions (e.g. Hinduism, yoga, judo, Taoist teachings, Zen philosophy, Japanese hai-kai). Suzi Frankl Sperber, in her work *Caos e cosmos*, besides supplying a list of supposedly all the books belonging to Ro-sa's library (in which Rosa's Asian titles are included), also writes a short chapter on the influence, in Rosa's literary pro-duction, of the Chandogya Upanishad (one of the oldest Upa-nishads, part of the collection of philosophical texts which form the theoretical basis for the Hindu religion) (57-63). In *Tutaméia* (1967), his last work published while still alive, Rosa confirms his interest in Zen Buddhism and, in particular, in the koan. The humor, the concision, the paradoxes, the absur-dity in *Tutaméia* are all characteristics of a writing done by a true koan master.

If I were to summarize this novel as a confessional[9] nar-rative, I could begin saying that GSV is a novel about Man's Fall and about Man's struggle to find the path back to the presence of the Divine. On a less metaphysical level, however, GSV is a reminiscence narrative articulated by the voice of an old farmer who, curiously and surprisingly, finds a "means" between a popular and an erudite style. Old Riobaldo, at the time of the narration, living comfortably on the banks of the great São Francisco River, in the state of Minas Gerais, Brazil, is the narrator of his own tale, in which young Riobaldo is the protagonist. Young Riobaldo's main adventures take place in the first decades of the 20th century, and start after he runs away from his (god)father's home. For the sake of his friend-ship with an enigmatic young man named Diadorim (whose true identity and gender are maintained veiled to the protag-onist, to the narratee as to us as well, by the narrator, until al-most to the very end of the narrative), Riobaldo joins a group of "mercenaries" (jagunços) headed by the honorable chief

---

9 'Confession' – as opposed to the memoir, for instance – implies that the speaker or writer wishes or even needs to reveal something that is hidden, possibly shameful, and difficult to articulate" (Herman 82).

Joca Ramiro. Riobaldo's narration speaks of young Riobaldo's ascension to the position of a great leader of a group of "jagunços" and their apocalyptic showdown with the hostile "jagunço" leader – Hermógenes – who carries throughout the narrative the stigma of being a Judas and a pact-maker (for being believed to have made a pact with the Devil). For some, GSV is a Faustian narrative because the theme of the pact with the Devil is of great concern for the old as well as the young Riobaldo.

My title for this chapter is itself connected to a minor character of GSV, Maria Mutema, who appears in one of the several interpolated stories within the novel. The importance of the "Mutema case" has been discussed by various critics as Rosa's address on Absolute Evil. Walnice Galvão refers to it as a "parable that speaks of pure evil" in *As formas do falso* (119). Utéza, as well, gives us a very detailed analysis of the Mutema case that underscores its importance within the novel (136-41). Maria Mutema, an inconspicuous wife living in the "sertão" (the backlands) of Minas, commits two atrocious crimes. First she kills her husband by pouring hot lead into his ear, and then she drives the village priest to his death by her insistent lies during her private confessions with him. My own reading of the case, without contradicting either Galvão's or Utéza's interpretations, has the intention of presenting it as a koan case in its literal definition. The crimes of Mutema become a "public record," "setting a standard of judgment"[10] (as in Fisher's literal definition of the koan cited above). Mutema serves as an Adamic archetype for the people of her community, and for us as well. "Without any motives"[11] she sins, and intuitively, she finds the path back to "the inner truth deeply hidden in [her] consciousness" (Suzuki 140): Mutema denies

---

10 "Confissão *edital,* consoantemente, para tremer *exemplo,* raio em pesadelo de quem ouvia, *público,* que rasgava gastura, como porque *avessava a ordem* das coisas e o quieto comum do viver transtornava" (GSV 313, my emphases).

11 "Que tinha matado o marido, aquela noite, *sem motivo nenhum, sem malfeito dele nenhum, causa nenhuma; por que, nem sabia*" (GSV 313, my emphases).

Evil and returns to God[12]. She stands by her own will before the Divine Court to be judged according to the Highest Principle. Mutema's case establishes for the citizens of her small village (a cosmos), the highest Principle for living, and their enlightenment (and her own) culminates with the redemption and almost beatification of Mutema.[13] Upon retelling this case, a story narrated by one of the "jagunços" (Jõe Bexiguento), old Riobaldo takes possession of its narrative as if it were his own story. The reason for Riobaldo's personal appropriation of the Mutema's narrative, I argue, has to do with personal affinities. Mutema's story is a microscopic mirror-image narrative of Riobaldo's own life's tale. As Mutema stood in sacred grounds before her whole village to confess, Riobaldo stands (or, more accurately, sits) before a public (the mysterious narratee he is narrating his tale to, and us, the readers), and in a verbal outburst initiates an obsessive and endless narration of quite a disturbing past. Fisher explains that

> [t]heoretically koans may take any form, but the most common consists of questions and answers [between masters and disciples] (mondo), stories or statements. One of the most famous koans is in the form of a *mondo*: The Master Jyoshii was once asked by a monk, 'Has a dog also Buddha nature or not?' Jyoshii said, 'Mu!' Mu (wit) was the character used by Zennists to translate the Sanskrit word *sunyata*, meaning "emptiness" or "devoid of self-nature". By means of koans, Zen Masters are able to convey the most important ideas, attitudes and conceptions of Zen Buddhism. (65)

In the famous koan just cited, "Mu" (emptiness) is the "punch

---

12 "E Maria Mutema, sozinha em pé, torta magra de preto, deu um gemido de lágrimas e exclamação, berro de corpo que faca estraçalha. *Pediu perdão! Perdão forte, perdão de fogo, que da dura bondade de Deus baixasse nela*" (GSV 313, my emphases).
13 "Mesmo, pela arrependida humildade que ela principiou, em tão pronunciado sofrer, alguns diziam que Maria Mutema estava ficando santa" (GSV 315).

line" (wato)[14]. The answer "Mu" (emptiness) is not the concept 'emptiness,' but the state of being absolutely empty. "To realize emptiness means to attain liberation. This is accomplished by purifying the mind of affirmation and negation" (Schuhmacher and Woerner 210). "An empty person allows all phenomena without discrimination to enter his or her experience and is totally unattached to anything in that experience" (Fenton 21). As Fisher points out, "Mu" "was the character for *sunyata* (enlightenment). Rosa's care in naming his characters manifests itself here: Mu-tema's case is about the "mu" theme, that is, about enlightenment. Rosa's "nonada" announces Rosa's exultant *satori* (enlightenment), a verbal explosion (very much like Master Jyoshii's "Mu!" and other Zen masters' alternate supplementary answers to the original koans, and indeed like Maria Mutema's) resulting from his contemplation and philosophical speculation[15] of a popular (Brazilian) superstition, which is put into a "koanish" magical formula by Rosa: "*O diabo na rua, no meio do redemoinho....*" [The devil in the street, in the middle of the whirlwind]. Walnice Galvão, on the one hand, labels Rosa's formula as an epigraph to the novel (129). Utéza, on the other, refers to this maxim as a subtitle to Rosa's novel and supplies us with its folkloric meaning, collected in L. Cascudo's *Dicionário do folclore brasileiro*, linking the whirlwind to the devil's vehicle of transport: "Quando se produz um redemoinho de vento, a que o povo da Beira Alta chama *borborinho*, acredita-se que então anda no ar o diabo, ou bruxas ou qualquer 'cousa má'" [When a whirlwind – or 'borborinho' as it is called by the people from Beira Alta – picks up, one believes that the devil is riding the air, or witches, or any evil] (Utéza 56-7). Apparently, this association with the devil is not unique to Brazilian and Portuguese cultural traditions. J. C. Cooper's *An Illustrated Encyclopaedia of Traditional Symbols* states under "whirlwind" its broader scope: "[in] wit-

---

14 Schuhmacher and Woerner 182
15 Rosa, in a letter dated May 21, 1958 to Vicente Ferreira da Silva, is cited to have written: 'Grande Sertão: Veredas' – que por bizarra que V. ache a afirmativa, é menos literatura pura do que um sumário de idéias e crenças do autor, [...]" (Martins 89).

chcraft it depicts the devil dancing with a witch and witches, wizards and evil spirits ride on whirlwinds" (192).

The full terms of my proposal, in this chapter, are that Rosa not only uses the Mutema's case as a koan to reflect on the existence and origin of Evil in the world, but also approaches his whirlwind motif, "The devil in the street, in the middle of the whirlwind," as a koan as well, in order to engage in a broader philosophical, theological and linguistic excursion on the same questions of Evil and mankind's road to Salvation. With the whirlwind koan, Rosa takes us to a surprising realization of ontological and linguistic (mis)perceptions.

"And in the beginning? How did Evil start?"[16] Riobaldo raises the unanswerable question. Even for Quelemém, Riobaldo's spiritual guide and an expert on Spiritism, that question turns out to be a riddle. The formula "O diabo na rua..." is frequently brought to the surface of the narrative by old Riobaldo, the narrator of the novel. Despite his unhesitant condemnation of and aloofness to the reigning superstition that surrounds him[17], as well as his categorical affirmation of the Devil's inexistence[18], old Riobaldo proceeds with caution when it comes to categorically denying its existence.[19] "The devil exists and does not exist?" puzzles old Riobaldo over his paradoxical discourse. GSV is a narrative that intends to withhold both ends of that question, an argument which requires a kind of logic that is non-logic within the criterion of the Cartesian discourse. Hence, Rosa's need for the (re)creation of a special language. Daisetz Teitaro Suzuki, in his book *Zen Buddhism*, wisely states that "[i]n the actual living of life there is no logic, for life is superior to logic" (151), and goes on to point out a few linguistic features in Zen Buddhist narratives, especially the koan, that reflect the Zennist epistemic

---

16 "Bem, mas o senhor dirá, deve de: e no começo – para pecados e artes, as pessoas – como por que foi que tanto emendado se começou? Ei, ei, aí todos esbarram" (GSV 12).

17 "Povo prascóvio" (GSV 3).

18 "E me inventei neste gosto, de especular idéia. O diabo existe e não existe? [...] Solto, por si, cidadão, é que não tem diabo nenhum" (GSV 6-7).

19 "Eu, pessoalmente, *quase* que já perdi nele a crença" (GSV 5, my emphasis).

and philosophical approach to life: paradox, going beyond opposites, contradiction, repetition, exclamation. Rosa, in my view, borrows these unique verbal recourses from the koan narrative style to engender a language which possibilitates his philosophical probing into the paradoxicality of his inquiry, i.e. makes his discourse possible.

What follows now is a comparison between the linguistic features of the koan narrative with the narrative of GSV. The intention in this comparison is to be exemplary rather than thematically exhaustive. "For Zen masters," says Hajime Nakamura, "the best way to express our deepest experiences is by the use of paradoxes which transcend the opposites" (108). "Do demo? Não gloso" [Over the devil? I do not gloss] affirms Riobaldo in a quite conspicuous manner in the very beginning of the second paragraph of the novel (GSV 4). A few pages later, he reiterates that intention. And yet, to define GSV as a narrative about Evil and the Devil, as many have done, is far from erroneous because it is about the Devil and Man, the devil in man. On the one hand, Riobaldo's self-contradictory statement of intentions (affirming not to talk about the devil, while obsessively talking about the devil), in simple terms, discloses the importance of the matter to him. "Este caso – por estúrdio que me vejam – é de minha certa importância. Tomara não fosse" [This case-as odd as it might seem – is of a certain importance to me. I wish it were not] (7). The secretive self-contradiction in Riobaldo's attitude begins to be comprehended only after the reader becomes acquainted with Riobaldo's tale: his youth's doubts and superstitions about the Devil's existence and pactual dealings. On the other hand, the self-contradiction might be deceptive. João Guimarães Rosa, a student of many languages, might be surreptitiously dealing with double meanings for the verb "glosar" (to gloss, to furnish glosses, commentaries of a text), but also, from the Scandinavian root "glossa" (to glow). The latter meaning gives us, in English, "to give a deceptively attractive appearance," which although unusual for Portuguese, cannot be discarded from Rosa's vocabulary. Creating the doubt was, probably, Rosa's intention. The paradox created is Rosa's warning to the reader of the double edge of language. Paradoxes abound on many of the pages of GSV, especially in references to God and the Devil, as in this brief example: "o diabo, é às brutas, mas Deus é traiçoeiro! Ah, uma beleza de traiçoeiro – dá gosto!" [the devil, he is rough-going, but God is deceiving! Ah, how beautifully deceiving He is – It makes one happy!] (22).

Continuing to cite from Nakamura's study on the koan language, the koan dialogues, different from the Platonic dialogues, required "no semantic connection between the questions and the answers. [...] They [the masters] gave answers in a figurative and intuitive way" (5). Dialogues are infrequent, but meaningful, in GSV. Questions and answers, both tend to be figurative. They only half-reveal their meaning. Unlike the mondo koan, in which the answer –sensical or nonsensical– follows immediately after the question, in GSV the answer to a question has usually a preamble of reflections that will lead the reader only intuitively to the answer. For example, in this idle exchange between Zé-Zim (a John Doe) and Riobaldo about raising guinea hens, the real target is one's individual need for inner changes. "Pergunto: – 'Zé-Zim, por que é que você não cria galinhas-d'angola, como todo o mundo faz?' – 'Quero criar nada não...' – me deu resposta: – 'Eu gosto muito de mudar...'" ["I ask: – 'Zé-Zim, why don't you raise guinea hens, like everybody else?' –'I donna want to raise anything...' –he gave me for an answer: – 'I like to be on the move...'"] (51). The double meaning of the verb "mudar" (to change and to move/to relocate) marks the pun. Proceeding with my comparison, Nakamura also comments that "[o]ne feature of Zen Buddhism is the penchant for the concrete expression of concepts" (115). The degree to which Rosa embraced the creative task of matching abstract ideas to concrete forms branded his discourse with a very unique poesy. An allegorical reading of GSV is not only possible, but to some extent has been done. Utéza's book, for example, structurally fulfills the function of matching Rosa's characters to Greek-Roman and Asian mythological personifications and archetypes. Utéza touches the allegorical aspects of some of the characters: in speaking of Zé Bebelo, Utéza very accurately names him "the Greek noos" (intelligence) (104). A favorite "allegory" in GSV, and a very important concept for the novel, is that of a "waterfall"[20] which, in my view, Rosa uses as a metaphor to discuss the possibility of the existence of the devil in the world. In Rosa's words, cited in the footnote below, a waterfall is a hill with water running over it. Take away the water (or the hill) and gone is the waterfall. Similarly, the devil is "man inside out" [o homem dos avessos]. Turn man outside in, i.e., back to man's original godly image, and there is no more devil. A koan is allegorical in the sense of rendering the intelligible through the sensible. What distinguishes it from most allegory (and brings it closer to the meaning of "symbol") is that the koan is meant to convey concepts that would otherwise remain beyond language. According to Dale S. Wright, "[s]acred formulas, devotional recitation of the thought or name of the Buddha, and visualization and conceptual 'contemplations' (kuan)," disseminated by the *Perfection of Wisdom Sutras* and the *Lotus Sutra*, "were forms of religious language that came to serve as the practical background for the development of the koan" (203). Furthermore, sacred formulas, "customarily recited in original or classical languages that are not understood by those who intone them in memorized form for ritual purposes [...] must be thought to possess a power not transferable into Chinese through translation and therefore ungraspable in concept" (203).

Rosa's broad knowledge of foreign languages naturally permeates his writing. His tendency is, however, to "baptize" the foreign words with familiar Portuguese sounds (prefixes, suffixes, spellings). Mary L. Daniel briefly comments on Rosa's "process of re-spelling" the adopted foreign words, and cites a few examples of foreign word borrowings within Rosa's novel such as the "English *swish* with reference to flowing water, taking advantage of the onomatopoeic quality of the word: Eu ambicionava o suíxo manso dum córrego nas lajes"

---

20 "O senhor vê: existe cachoeira; e pois? Mas cachoeira é barranco de chão, e água se caindo por ele, retombando; o senhor consome essa água, ou desfaz o barranco, sobra cachoeira alguma? Viver é negócio muito perigoso.... Explico ao senhor: o diabo vige dentro do homem, os crespos do homem – ou é o homem arruinado, ou o homem dos avessos" (GSV 7).

(96). There are sacred formulas being evoked, and also being recommended[21] in GSV. Despite of all their words being in Portuguese, the full meaning of the formulas gets lost in their hermeticism. At midnight, at the stipulated place of his supposed encounter with the devil, the Veredas Tortas, Riobaldo evokes a sacred formula, calling upon himself courage to face the devil: "fôlego de fôlego de fôlego – da mais-força, de maior-coragem. A que vem, tirada a mando, de setenta e setentas distâncias do profundo mesmo da gente" [breath from breath from breath – of the greatest strength, of the greatest courage. Courage that is drawn upon command from seventy plus seventy distances of the deepest within us] (600). Repetitious words and numerology is, of course, part of the magical package.[22] Devotional recitation is also present in the narrative of GSV. Instead of "imagining the Buddha and reciting his name," Riobaldo summons a Christian version of Siddhartha Gautama – Joca Ramiro (a supposed avatar of Christ in the novel), by invoking his name for protection[23] against the "monster Hermógenes."

Besides linguistic features, there are also spiritual concepts inside the koan narratives, which Rosa has transposed into the language of GSV, allowing them to manifest through syntax, semantics, and orthography. According to G. Victor Sogen Hori, upon entering the monasteries, the monks "receive their first koan, usually the 'Sound of one hand' or 'Joshu's Mu,'" (288) which they usually pass within a year. In addition:

---

21 "Compadre meu Quelemém, muitos anos depois, me ensinou que todo desejo a gente realizar alcança – se tiver ânimo para cumprir, sete dias seguidos, a energia e paciência forte de só fazer o que dá desgosto, nojo, gastura e cansaço, e de rejeitar toda qualidade de prazer" (GSV 210-11).

22 "The greatest mathematical philosophers of ancient Babylonia and Greece, and later, India, believed that numbers could reveal the principles of creation and the laws of space and time" (Tresidder 346). The number seven, in particular, is considered "a sacred, mystical and magic number, especially in the traditions of western Asia, symbolizing cosmic and spiritual order and the completion of a natural cycle" (Tresidder 433).

23 "Pensei nele só, forte. Pensando: – 'Joca Ramiro! Joca Ramiro! Joca Ramiro!...'" (GSV 279).

[T]hey are told to answer the koan by 'becoming one' with it. 'Become one with…' is an important concept [in Zen teaching]. [It means] 'to become the thing itself.' The proper way to chant sutras, to chop vegetable, to sit in meditation is to become the sutra-chanting itself, to become the act of chopping, etc. It means to perform one's work without indulging in subject – object duality. (Hori 297 – 99)

Rosa's masterly linguistic skill to disclose the awareness of "become one with" can be perceived, for example, in the simplicity of Riobaldo's phrase: "eu, sentinela!"[24], a clever "twofold truth and pun" (Hori 301), another common linguistic characteristic between the koan and GSV narratives. Unfortunately lost in translation, "I, the sentinel!" (eu, sentinela!) unfolds into a higher truth: "I felt in her" (Eu senti nela). The "jagunço" chief, young Riobaldo, learns from the prostitute Maria-da-Luz the grace of sharing with the lower-ranked Felisberto the enjoyment of his (Riobaldo's) prostitutes. "I" (chief) and "the Other" (sentinel) become one, or "I become one with the Other."

GSV is a philosophical, theological, and spiritual excursion into the existence *and* inexistence of Evil. Rosa, as well as Riobaldo, is fully aware of the nature of this speculation.[25] Linguistically, that is through the spermatic power of language, Rosa makes the Devil (*demo*) exist right in the center of the whirlwind (re-*demo*-inho) only to adamantly deny Its existence: "Solto, por si, cidadão, é que não tem diabo nenhum." [Free, as an entity of his own, for sure there is no devil] (7). This contradiction is only one of the many occasions in which we witness the non-logical character of Rosa's narrative language, another characteristic that GSV shares with the koan

---

24 "O senhor sabe: eu chefe, o outro sentinela. […] Sendo o mais que pensei: eu, sentinela! O senhor sabe. Ah – ainda que no nocivo desses andares – eu conseguia meditar minhamente: ah, eu não tive os chifres-chavelhos nem os pés de cabra…" (GSV 757).
25 "[…] estou de range rede. E me inventei neste gosto, de especular idéia" (GSV 6).

narrative. "When Chao-chou (c. 850 A.D.) was asked 'Does the Buddha nature exist in a dog?' he answered in the affirmative on one occasion and in the negative on another. [...] The reasons for these contradictory answers are to be found in the concrete situations which elicited them" (Nakamura 3-6). In GSV, Riobaldo affirms categorically that "everything is and is not."[26] The Devil does not exist. However, on It is bestowed, throughout the novel, 73 different names (Castro 68), one more than the Judeo-Christian tradition of attributing 72 names to God. Rosa's linguistic liberation from the logic of duality allows apparently "nonsensical" constructions like Riobaldo's boast: "A prova minha, era que o Demônio mesmo sabe que ele não há, só por só, que carece de existência" ["My proof was that the devil himself knows that he does not exist on his own, and needs existence"] (670), or like Riobaldo's lament: "Digo ao senhor: o diabo não existe, não há, e a ele eu vendi a alma... Meu medo é este" [I tell you: the devil does not exist, there is none, but it was to him that I sold my soul...This is my fear] (693). Hori states that

> [i]n the conventional realm in which we normally reside, we usually abide by the rules of Either/Or logic, the logic of duality. Here if we make a statement, implying that it is true, we are also implying that its negation is false. However, according to the Vimalakirti Sutra, in the realm of the "inconceivable liberation", through the Dharma-door of non-duality (297), this dualistic logic does not work. In this [latter] realm, it is possible to make contradictory statements. The bodhisattvas[27] Vimalakirti and Manjusri, both of whom reside in the 'inconceivable liberation', converse in such contradictions.

---

26 "O senhor ache e não ache. Tudo é e não é..." (GSV 9).

27 Bodhisattva: "enlightenment being; a being who seeks buddhahood through the systematic practice of the perfect virtues, but renounces complete entry into nirvana until all beings are saved" (Schuhmacher and Woerner 39).

'-Welcome, Manjusri! You are very welcome. There you are, without any coming. You appear, without any seeing. You are heard, without any hearing.' Manjusri declared, 'Householder, it is as you say. Who comes, finally comes not. Who goes, finally goes not. Why? Who comes is not known to come. Who goes is not known to go. Who appears is finally not to be seen.' – In this realm, what we normally take to be opposites are made identical: form is emptiness and emptiness is form. [...] These statements appear to conventional understanding as examples of a different kind of logic, the logic of Both/And. *Both* a statement *and* its opposite are true. (Hori 299)

There is no doubt that Rosa is scattering the "logic of non-duality" throughout Riobaldo's narrative. It is quite exposed in the motif "Everything is *and* is not." It shows up in other occasions as well. For example, Rosa's ludic trick with the verbs "ensinar" (to teach) and "aprender" (to learn) hides the seriousness of his intention in this brief dialogic exchange between Zé Bebelo and Riobaldo[28]: "Tu foi o meu discípulo... Foi não foi?" [You were my disciple, were you not?] – "A bom, eu não te ensinei; mas bem te aprendi a saber certa a vida..." [I did not teach you; but I learned you well to know what is right in life...] (827). As in the conversation between the two bodhisattvas, Vimalakirti and Manjusri, opposites are made identical; "ensinar" and "aprender" become one and the same verb, consequently erasing the dualistic distinction between the grammatical "subject" and "object." Zé Bebelo and Riobaldo become, simultaneous and interchangeably, "subject" and "object" with the fusion of the two verbs. In the non-dualistic linguistic realm of GSV, both (Riobaldo and Zé Bebelo)

---

28 " – 'Há-te! Acabou com o Hermógenes? A bem. Tu foi o meu discípulo... Foi não foi?'
Deixei: ele dizer [...]– 'A bom, eu não te ensinei; mas bem te aprendi a saber certa a vida...' Eu ri, de nós dois" (GSV 872).

are, simultaneously, masters to and disciples of each other.

According to Suzuki, "Zen mistrusts the intellect, does not rely upon traditional and dualistic methods of reasoning, and handles problems after its own original manners." (56). Rosa dealt with his whirlwind koan (The devil in the street…) in the Zen way. Whirlwinds appear throughout GSV, sometimes clearly defined, others disguisedly. Rosa's epistemic approach to his koan (O diabo na rua…), as well as to the linguistic discourse in which he narrated the novel, reflects the elusive quality of his whirlwind: orthodox and unorthodox; ominous and humorous; devilish and divine. As stated earlier, Cooper's *Encyclopaedia* speaks of the devilish association of whirlwinds. However, under the same entry, it clearly connects whirlwinds to the divine: "Circular, solar and creative movement. Whirlwinds were regarded as a manifestation of energy in nature, rising from a center of power associated with gods, supernatural forces and entities who travel on whirlwinds, or speak from them" (192). Traditionally, it seems that the exoteric meaning of whirlwinds carries association with evil powers, while to an esoteric's eyes, they are always connected to divine powers. The swastika, an ideogram associated with the whirlwind (Cooper 164-166), represents cosmic dynamism and creative energy and appears on the footprint or breast of the Buddha. It is also a sign of Christ moving in the world (Tresidder 459-60). Kabbalists explain the process of creation of the world through divine manifestations, which are represented in ten sefirot (spheres). Keter (crown) is the supernal sphere, the point from which the whole created universe manifests. The swastika is a symbol for Keter. Keter is described as "the first swirlings [sic] of manifestation" (Wang 55). Rosa is interested in the dual speculation of this popular image, i.e. the diabolical and destructive as well as the divine and creative powers of this spiral force. In a "Mu" state of mind ("purified of affirmation and negation"),[29] Rosa goes about his speculation in both a humorous and ominous tone.

---

29 See previous citation from Schuhmacher and Woerner 210.

There are three major encounters with whirlwinds in the novel. Young Riobaldo's first encounter, which is with a real whirlwind, distinguishes itself for its light and humorous tone. This is a prolepsis though, an anticipation of the two later, and more crucial, encounters. Riobaldo's horse, Siruiz, gets startled by a whirlwind and almost throws the rider off its back.[30] The "devil" inside the whirlwind turns out to be a leaf. Rosa's careful description of the scene is justified later, by the two other major incidents with whirlwinds, when all the elements used here are brought back, but in totally different scenarios. We have, in this scene, two testimonies: on one end is Caçange, who immediately identifies the devil's presence in the funnel[31]; on the other is Diadorim, who explains the funnel as "twisted wind that comes from the sea."[32] Young Riobaldo stands in between these two views, as uneasy as his horse, unsure of his own laugh. Old Riobaldo darkens the lighthearted narration in the end of the episode, with a foreboding warning to the narratee (the mysterious man listening to Riobaldo's narrative): "[O] senhor nunca deve de renovar" [You should never repeat those words][33] (342). Probably unnoticed by most readers is Diadorim's connecting of the whirlwind to the sea, a reference to a metaphoric "sea" (source of life and creation) since the state of Minas is not on the coast.

In young Riobaldo's second major encounter with a whirlwind, we have a repetition of the compositional elements of the scene of the first encounter: "The devil in the street" magic formula; the whirlwind; the "ro-ro" of the wind; and even the humor (Riobaldo walking around in pitch dark, calling for the devil). The perspective has changed dramatically, though. Young Riobaldo is at Veredas Tortas, place and time of the encounter with the devil. He, who in the previous

---

30 "E o que era, que estava assombrando o animal, era uma folha seca esvoaçada, que sobre se viu quase nos olhos e nas orelhas dele. Do vento. Do vento que vinha, rodopiado. Redemoinho: o senhor sabe – a briga de ventos" (GSV 341).

31 "– 'Redemonho!' – o Caçanje falou, esconjurando" (GSV 342).

32 " – 'Vento que enviesa, que vinga da banda do mar...' – Diadorim disse" (GSV 342).

33 "Acho o mais terrível da minha vida, ditado nessas palavras, que o senhor nunca deve de renovar" (GSV 342).

scene was outside the funnel and unable to see inside, now wishes himself inside the funnel face to face with the devil. "Nós dois, e o tornopio do pé-de-vento" [Both of us and the twist of the funnel] (600). We can appreciate Rosa's linguistic difficulties in narrating this encounter: How to narrate an encounter with someone who is and is not? Plotinus, in his discourses about God (the One), used the "via negativa" to speak of the One. For Plotinus, the One exists, but the One's infinity is beyond the finitude of language. Hence, Plotinus resorted to negative language to describe what the One is not.[34] For Rosa, nevertheless, God *is*..., and all His attributes should be rendered to Him. "Deus é grande!"(418), "Deus é alegria e coragem – que Ele é bondade" (440), "Deus é uma plantação" (481). As Riobaldo points out, the problem lies with this world: "Ao que, este mundo é muito misturado..." [This world is all mixed up] (307). Things are and are not. In Riobaldo's (as well as Rosa's) voice, one hears a profound lament for the loss of power of words, and a plea to protect their sacredness: "Nome de lugar onde alguém já nasceu, devia de estar sagrado" [The name of a place where someone was born should become sacred] (52). Rosa's only linguistic salvation is to resort to the logic of the bodhisattvas, the logic of non-duality. Rosa's narration of Riobaldo's non-encounter with the devil ends up sounding a lot like the bodhisattvas' encounter from the citation above.[35] [And something that was not coming. I was not seeing something that was strange to my eyes. That, which was not coming, the gust of a gale, with Him on the throne, in profile, stately sitting in the center.]

---

34   "The One is ineffable. Language will never disclose the One: "How then do we speak about it [the One]? Indeed we say something about it, but we do not say the One itself." (V.3.14.1-3) "Yet we may use language to speak about, or discuss the One, so long as we are aware of the limitations of speech. The project of negative theology has as its goal to make language do things that it normally would not do while observing appropriate caveats at each stage of its progress toward the one. Negative theology is not an expression of mystical silence, but is always a function of speech used in the service of philosophy" (Gerson 344).

35 "E qualquer coisa que não vinha. Não vendo estranha coisa de se ver. Ao que não vinha – a lufa de um vendaval grande, com Ele em trono, contravisto, sentado de estadela bem no centro" (GSV 599).

Young Riobaldo's third significant encounter with a whirlwind is again a repetition of the basic compositional elements of the first encounter with a new perspective. This time Riobaldo looks into the funnel from above. What does he see? The "devil," Hermógenes, in a deathly combat with Diadorim, the "angel." This is, in my opinion, the climax as well as the most misunderstood scene of the novel. And Rosa planned it that way. It is a problem of (mis)perception. Traditionally, we perceive the Devil as a destructive force and Death as an end to life. For Rosa, I believe, considering his background knowledge of esoteric religions (Cabbalah, Spiritism) and Asian philosophies (Taoism, Zen-Buddhism), his perception of this scene is reversed. According to kabbalist tradition, stated by Robert Wang, "the Devil does not exist"; "All things were from One, by the meditation of One"; "[T]here is nothing in the universe not of God, including the so called Devil" (172); "Evil is unbalanced force. It is a by-product of evolution, resulting from a stage of temporary imbalance. Unity is the ultimate good, and unity is the result of the balance of two opposites" (55); "[B]irth and death are essentially the same transition" (181). The third whirlwind, in appearance the most destructive and tragic one, is on the contrary, like the taiji (Yin and Yang), a harmonic union of two polar forces. Where the exoteric eye sees destruction, the esoteric eye sees the beginning of creation. Diadorim, who stands for the divine, goodness, light, and beauty unites through death with Hermógenes, the image of evil, darkness, and deformity. As in the case of Yin and Yang, universal harmony is reached with the union of opposites.

"Solving a koan requires a leap to another level of comprehension […], an intuitive leap, which takes [the student] into a world beyond logical contradictions and dualistic modes of thought" (Schuhmacher and Woerner 182). This is the leap into "Nonada" of GSV, a space somewhere in the labyrinths of Rosa's sertão (desert) and his veredas (rivers). There, Rosa untwists the twisted meanings of his whirlwind in search of the Highest Principle. In the end of life, old

Riobaldo expresses his wisdom through a smart word pun[36] that says that one lives to be disillusioned—that is, to be disenchanted—but the under-meaning intended is to free oneself from the illusions of life. Reality is not always what we perceive. Sometimes, it is the reverse of our (mis)perceptions. The "demo" (devil) or the "medo" (fear – an anagram for demo) in the middle of the "redemoinho" (whirlwind) we are riding on hinders our full perception of reality because, inside it, things are all mixed; the "demo" of the "redemoinho" stands for devilish destruction as well as divine creation. Stepping out of the spiral (as Riobaldo did in his third encounter with a whirlwind) for a full view of our inner "cosmos" just might reveal to us reality's real face. Sometimes, it takes a whole living to find the formula for living. But it exists, Riobaldo assures us.

BIBLIOGRAPHY

Bluteau, Rafael. "A letra elementar portugueza e scientífica." *Instituto de Estudos Brasileiros*. Universidade de São Paulo, n.d. Web. 4 Jul 2012.

Castro, Nei Leandro de. *Universo e vocabulário do Grande sertão*. Rio de Janeiro: José Olympio, 1970. Print.

Cooper, J.C. *An Illustrated Encyclopaedia of Traditional Symbols*. London: Thames and Hudson, 1999. Print.

Daniel, Mary L. "Word Formation and Deformation in 'Grande Sertão: Veredas.'" *Luso-Brazilian Review* 2.1 (1965): 81-97. Print.

Fenton, John Y., et al. *Religions of Asia*. New York: St. Martin's Press, 1988. Print.

Ferreira, Aurélio Buarque de Holanda. *Novo dicionário da língua portuguesa*. Rio de Janeiro: Editora Nova Fronteira, 1975. Print.

Fisher, John F. "An Analysis Of The Koans In The Mu Mon Kwan." *Numen* 25.1 (Apr. 1978): 65-76. Print.

Galvão, Walnice Nogueira. *As formas do falso*. São Paulo: Editora Perspectiva, 1972. Print.

---

36   "A gente vive, eu acho, é mesmo para se desiludir e desmisturar" (GSV 200).

Gerson, Lloyd P., ed. *The Cambridge Companion to Plotinus*. Cambridge: Cambridge University Press, 1999. Print.

Herman, David et al, eds. *Routledge Encyclopedia of Narrative Theory*. New York: Routledge, 2008. Print.

Hori, G. Victor Sogen. "Koan and Kensho in the Rinzai Zen Curriculum." *The Koan: Texts and Contexts in Zen Buddhism*. Ed. Steven Heine and Dale S. Wright. Cary, NC: Oxford University Press, 2000. 280-315. Print.

Martins, Heitor. *Do barroco a Guimarães Rosa*. Belo Horizonte, Brazil: Editora Itatiaia, 1983. Print.

Miura, Isshu, and Ruth Fuller Sasaki. *Zen dust the history of the koan and koan study in Rinzai (Lin-chi) Zen*. New York: Harcourt, Brace & World, 1966. Print.

Nakamura, Hajime. "The Non-Logical Character of Zen." *Journal of Chinese Philosophy* 12 (1985): 105-115. Print.

Rosa, João Guimarães. *Tutaméia*. Rio de Janeiro: Editora Nova Fronteira S.A., 2001. Print.

—. *Grande Sertão: Veredas*. Rio de Janeiro: Editora Nova Aguilar, 1994. Print.

Schuhmacher, Stephan, and Gert Woerner, eds. *The Encyclopedia of Eastern Philosophy and Religion: Buddhism, Hinduism, Taoism, Zen*. Boston: Shambhala, 1994. Print.

Sperber, Suzi Frankl. *Caos e cosmos: leituras de Guimarães Rosa*. São Paulo: Livraria Duas Cidades, 1976. Print.

Suzuki, Daisetz T. *Zen Buddhism: Selected Writings of D.T.Suzuki*. Ed. William Barrett. Westminster, MD: Doubleday Publishing, 1996. Print.

Tresidder, Jack, ed. *The Complete Dictionary of Symbols*. San Francisco: Chronicle Books, 2005. Print.

Utéza, Francis. *João Guimarães Rosa: metafísica do grande sertão*. São Paulo: Edusp, 1994. Print.

Wang, Robert. *The Qabalistic Tarot: A Textbook of Mystical Philosophy*. Columbia, MD.: Marcus Aurelius Press, 2004. Print.

Wright, Dale S. "Koan History – Transformative Language in Chinese Buddhist Thought." *The Koan: Texts and Contexts in Zen Buddhism*. Ed. Steven Heine and Dale S. Wright. Cary, NC: Oxford University Press, 2000. 200-12. Print.

Part two:

Spanish-middle eastern orientalisms

Hybrid Language and Space: Tensions Between Orientalism and Occidentalism in Mohamed Akalay's *Entre Tánger y Larache*

Kenneth Yanes

At the crossroads of Africa, the Middle East, and Europe a diversity of cultures flourishes within Morocco. In this country one finds the relics of a multifaceted past founded on the autochthonous cultures of the Amazigh (Berber) tribes, followed by the Roman Empire, Islam through the Arab conquest, and the Spanish and French protectorates at the beginning of the 20th century. These vestiges are evident in Morocco's sociolinguistic landscape today, especially within the Moroccan Arabic vernacular, Darija, with lexical influences from Tamazight Berber, French, and Castilian. Darija is used on a daily basis alongside Standard Modern Arabic (*Fus'ha*), French, and Castilian (depending on the region of the country). This linguistic hybridization is an analogy of the contemporary geography and space of a Moroccan citizen. Amazigh tribes bequeathed the longstanding systems of gendered space: public space is that of a man and the interior is that of a woman. With the new socioeconomic demands that followed the industrial era, European colonization, and a wave of immigration, these spatial systems have become progressively frustrated until causing a veritable inversion at the moment Moroccans immigrated to the West.

It is not surprising, then, that one cannot claim to find a singular form of Moroccan literature, as there are many which are primarily distinguished through the language of expression. Currently, one can find a growth of literature and journalism in Darija, and in the academic fields one finds a constant predilection for Modern Standard Arabic and French. English is also gaining its presence through the globalization of the market of North Africa. Literary expression in Castilian, however, has been exclusively reserved for the north of the country and only among a select group of journalists and academics that have remained active in cities such as Tangier, Larache, and Tetuan. This group is formed exclusively of men that continue a tradition of educating themselves through Western literature and thought; they read Marx, Gramsci, Molière, Racine, Cervantes, Bécquer, etc. One writer from this group, Mohamed Akalay, was a key figure in the establishment of the *Asociación de Escritores Marroquíes en Lengua Española* (AEMLE), founded in 1997, where he currently serves as the President of the Association.

In this study I will focus chiefly on a collection of short stories by Mohamed Akalay, *Entre Tánger y Larache* (2006), which, in my opinion, clearly depicts the tensions that exist within the hybrid language and space of Moroccans today. Akalay's work presents his audience with a dialogue that thrives between the Orient and the Occident in which a Moroccan appropriates the Castilian language because, as Cristián Ricci suggests, (beyond the mere fact of a Moroccan writing in Castilian in order to be understood) the Moroccan writes from the "other side of the periphery" when comparing him or herself to the Latin American writer, whose language was also acquired through Spanish imperialism (*Literatura periférica* 32).

This appropriation of the Castilian language does not come without its complications. Akalay's collection of short stories presents a conflict of style between Moroccan *costumbrista* literature – didactic and moralizing with its roots in Arabic oral traditions – and Western literature with an esthetic tradition rooted in elements of metaphor, symbolism, allusions, orientalism, etc. Contemporary Moroccan literature descends from past traditions of *costumbrista* literature, nearly journalistic realism, and historical annals that document the plight of the migrants (Ricci, "Moroccan Literature" 196). Ricci posits that modern day writers such as Akalay are a part of

> a fourth group that proliferated in the last seven years, and that in my view, will place Moroccan literature written in Castilian within the framework of a literature without boarders. This literature, written in Morocco by Moroccans, with Moroccan topics and characteristics, is developing a series of questions about the use of language of the Other,

the aesthetic practices of Western literature, and a deeply critical observation on the influence of the Western media on Morocco. (196)

Akalay's readers (as the characters in his works) are dispersed on both sides of the Strait of Gibraltar. Moroccan writers of Castilian expression maintain the *costumbrista* tradition for their Moroccan readers, who are filled with moralizing fables, proverbs from the Qu'ran, and realism of the daily life, a life that leads many to the decision of leaving to find a better life in the West. While writing to a Spanish or Western audience, these writers aim to incorporate literary esthetics with the *costumbrista* tradition; it is here where one finds the occidentalization of Moroccan literature.

Through the use of Homi Bhabha's theory of *mimesis* and Edward Said's theory on the reception of orientalism, Ricci posits that writers such as Akalay take the risk of auto-orientalizing themselves when they not only write in Castilian, but *as* a Spaniard for the purpose of gaining more attention (marketability) and being understood on the other side of the Strait of Gibraltar ("Moroccan literature" 196). It is the access to a world outside of Morocco through literature, but its reception in the Western world will not occur matter-of-factly. Ricci adds:

> However, like in all worlds, there are different levels of cultural citizenship. In order to avoid being a 'literary wetback,' these writers would have to fulfill at least two guidelines: to begin writing what the Western market is consuming at the moment, or to be exotic, magical, and sensual enough to captivate the Western reader, 'always eager and restless for romanticism' (Said 10). In order to avoid this literary submission to the West, Moroccan writers should begin a new critical vision of their peripheral culture with respect to Europe (and to the United States). (196)

These "levels of cultural citizenship" also translate into levels

59

of marketability of Moroccan literature in Castilian as Ricci argues in his article (196). This "peripheral" Moroccan culture within the West (outside of Morocco) is a *space* for hybridity and there is no other way to progress but to expose this hybridity that is occurring and expanding on a daily basis in communities of Spain, France, and the rest of the Western world. This is the reality of the immigrant that lives on the periphery of Western cultural hegemonies. To expose this peripheral culture cogently to the West is the main challenge, but to achieve this successfully would jet Moroccan literature in Castilian into the fore of the literary world. It would be a moment of discovery for the West as they read of a parallel world occurring *within* its own.

This moment of confrontation between West and East in the form of hybridity (as found in Moroccan literature in Castilian), however, is not the first occurrence in the history of Castilian-language literature. José Cadalso's *Cartas marruecas*, published seven years after his death in 1789, is a moment of literary hybridity in which Cadalso speaks through his Moroccan protagonist, Gazel, who in the novel is writing a set of epistles to friends and family. After his travels throughout Europe, he settles in Spain as part of the Moroccan ambassador's retinue from where he writes back mostly to his adoptive father back in Morocco on the Spanish "national character" as compared to other nations of Europe. This is Cadalso's decisive moment to share a critical vision of Spain through a hybridity of voice and style, which he explains in his introduction:

> Alguna de ellas [las cartas] mantienen todo el estilo, y aun el genio, digámoslo así, de la lengua arábiga su original; parecerán ridículas sus frases a un europeo, sublimes y pindáricas contra el carácter del estilo epistolar y común; pero también parecerán inaguantables nuestras locuciones a un africano. ¿Cuál tiene razón? ¡No lo sé! [...] Es demasiada la confusión de otras voces para que se oiga la de la común madre en muchos asuntos de los que se presentan en el trato diario de los hombres. (79)

In order for this literary moment of hybridity to be credible to Cadalso's readers, he explains that an acquaintance bequeathed the collection of epistles to him before dying. It is in the introduction to *Cartas marruecas* where he develops a crucial question of reception from East to West and from West to East, pertinent to and not unlike Ricci's argument on the issues concerning the reception of Moroccan literature in Castilian in the Castilian-speaking West. Cadalso argues that though the Arabic style might seem ridiculous to a European, a European style might seem unbearable to an African. He is left baffled and leaves the argument defeated by simply admitting that he does not know which style is better. Moreover, what his readers do not know is that he had to orientalize himself in order to speak through Gazel. He had to assume the gaze of the Other in order to approach a critical view of his own society. I posit, following Ricci's suggestions for modern Moroccan literature, that writers such as Akalay are following a similar, if not identical, paradigm of hybridity as Cadalso. They must in some way assume some facet of the Occidental gaze—that of the Castilian language in the case of Akalay—in order to form a critical view of the space and geography of his peripheral culture within the West as a bicultural/immigrant/Other. The challenge, again, is to propagate their literature to the West, as Cadalso did through his literary ruse, and to do so without compromising their Moroccaness.

A theory of intercultural communication states that the social marginality of the bicultural individual only allows him or her to live *within* "the margins" of two social contexts (Bennett 1993). It is necessary to emphasize that this theory does not address the issue of social marginalization (I will not discuss marginalization in this case as it is the Other who is *actively* assuming the Castilian language), but that of a social agility that allows frequent switching between social contexts on a quotidian basis. Moroccans live within various structures of social marginality, but, as Bennett's theory continues to suggest (120), there will always be a culture that is more dominant over the others within the context of social marginality. I posit that it is this tension, born out of the necessity of a dominant culture, which shapes contemporary Moroccan literature expressed in Castilian. In her article "Purity, Impurity, and Separation," philosopher Maria Lugones also forms a theory of *mestizaje* and identity in which she juxtaposes the process of "separation" or "curdling" when two seemingly "pure" and distinct elements are mixed. Lugones challenges the concept of "impurity" of identity and gives agency to the *mestizo* or bicultural individual to define him or herself:

> Curdle-separation is not something that happens to us but something we do. As I have argued, it is something we do in resistance to the logic of control, to the logic of purity. Though transparents fail to see its sense, and thereby keep its sense from structuring our social life, that we curdle testifies to our being active subjects, not consumed by the logic of control. Curdling may be haphazard technique of survival as an active subject, or it can become an art of resistance, metamorphosis, transformation. (478)

Does biculturalism, therefore, mean that one has to give into a "dominant" culture, perhaps that of the colonizer, or does it simply mean that one has the agency to chose and amplify whatever aspects of the two cultures we seem to naturally assume? How does a writer such as Akalay simultaneously address a Moroccan public and a Western public without having one culture dominate over the other within his or her writing? If Lugones' theory of "individual purity" stands, then who is at odds with hybridity and who is creating the tensions between Occidentalism and Orientalism? Is it the author, the Moroccan reader or the Western reader?

Mohamed Akalay's collection of ten short stories, *Entre Tánger y Larache*, is one of his first works to be published in Spain through Sial/Casa de África in 2006, which awarded him the collection's prize for best narrative that same year. The prologue, written by Cristián Ricci, opens by affirming that Akalay's choice of expression through short stories is nothing arbitrary, but rather a direct inheritance of Moroccan and Arabic literary tradition, which is didactic, moralizing, and adherent to the traditions and sayings of the Qu'ran (7). Akalay's stories observe a stark "social realism" that bares witness to the ever-evolving ways of life of Moroccans – and to some extent of all people in the Islamic world – which include themes such as unfulfilled marriages, the role of women in modern society, family and children, death and widowhood, terrorism, poverty, and the need for immigration and its devastation of the collective morale of the Moroccan people (8). Within the stories of the lives of Akalay's characters, one does indeed find the tensions between Orientalism and Occidentalism, that of social marginality and biculturalism on both sides of the Strait of Gibraltar, which leads to the hybridization of the language and space observed in these stories.

Almost all of Akalay's stories occur in a space that is hardly ever contained within a town, a city, or even Morocco itself. The reality of another world across the Strait of Gibraltar seems ever present and looming with proposals of marriage, usually when a man who is educated, employed, and socially "integrated" into European society seeks to take his Moroccan bride back with him. Such is the case in the first story of the collection, "Casamiento frustrado," in which we find a single, educated, and desirable young woman, Hind, whose parents are eager and hopeful to see their daughter married off to a man. He, however, cannot be just *any* man: he should respect her, let her have the freedom to develop her life and who will, of course, provide for her without cheating or shaming her, be it in Morocco or abroad. Hind would have the right to choose whom she will marry, though it is still customary to ask the father of the bride for her hand in marriage. When approached with a marriage proposition from family members on behalf of a young man named Hamid, who is living in France. As opposed to having the young man present himself in person before Hind's father, Hind's father, el Hadj, does *not* find it odd that a proposal involves the prospects of having his daughter move to France.

Today it would be considered very common for a young Moroccan woman to move to Europe for marriage; one could even say that it could be preferable for some families. As one observes in the story, dowries and financial stability are not the sole concerns of Hind's father as he converses with Hamid's father, sidi (sir) Talbi:

> —Dígame una cosa, sidi Talbi; ¿Hamid ha estado alguna vez casado o está casado en el presente?
> —Mi hijo es soltero. Tiene un gran futuro en Francia. Es ingeniero y trabaja en una importante empresa de construcción. Su hija tendrá todo lo que desee...
> —A mi hija, gracias a Dios, nunca le ha faltado de nada; por lo que el dinero no es lo importante. Lo que un padre pide es que su hija sea respetada y querida.
> —Con mi hijo Hamid tendrá lo que usted señala...
> —Permítanme decirles que no puedo darles una contestación ahora. Tendré que consultarlo con mi hija, decirle quién es su pretendiente; si ella acepta, se lo diré a ustedes. (15)

The father quite clearly has his qualms about this mysterious suitor who shows interest in his daughter from abroad. With the hybrid space of such an international marriage proposal comes what appears to be the evolution (that perhaps can be a source of tension) of a woman's agency in Moroccan culture. The expansion and hybridization of space, was, at its start, highly gendered in North African culture and is now allowing women to step out of the confines of the closed, intimate and subjugated feminine spaces, enough for her to chose whom she will marry and if her partner will make *her* happy. This can arguably be the effect of Moroccan-European biculturalism or a new movement of urban Moroccan women who are educated and can provide for themselves, which now even impacts the role of the patriarch in the life of a woman.

As the plot of the story unfolds, one is also confronted with the question of the hybridization of Akalay's language, which also brings his literary style into question. Throughout his short stories, one finds his command of the Castilian language to be more than capable of creating moving and poetic narratives within his almost journalistic realism, through which he makes his reader confront the realities of modern Moroccan society. Within what seems to be a heavily occidentalized style of realism, one finds that there is a convergence with the metaphysical, the fantastic, and the magical. As mentioned above, Hind's story leads to the discovery of the intentions behind the enigmatic marriage proposal sent from France. Her parents discuss their qualms and Hind's mother loses no time to visit a seer (*vidente*), who, through visions of drowned and mutilated animals, comes to certain conclusions regarding Hind's suitor:

> —Antes voy a decirte lo que hay. Acabo de recibir unas imágenes que demuestran que ese hombre está casado. Para que te asegures, te pido que busques a un familiar que tiene en la ciudad; ese hombre te dirá la verdad. Las visiones que he tenido son las siguientes… Y el vidente le contó con todo detalle a la mujer las visiones recibidas.
> —¿Cómo sabe usted que ese hombre está casado?
> —Te lo voy a explicar. Ese hombre estaba casado con dos mujeres; al cabo de un tiempo decidió repudiar a una de ella; el mal rato que conoció esa señora la llevó a la muerte. La otra siguió con él. Ahora es su mujer…. (17)

Hind's mother follows the seer's instructions and finds an estranged member of Hamid's family, Nuredin Asili, who was able to confirm all of what the seer explained. Hamid was indeed a dishonest man who lived abroad and made money by abducting young women for ransom under the guise of a marriage proposal. Nuredin goes farther to explain that Hamid's branch of the family is entirely corrupt. Hind and her family are spared from the tragedy that would have occurred should she have moved to France with Hamid.

How does this fantastical episode then fit in Akalay's stark social realism? One would have to turn towards a system of Moroccan beliefs of the supernatural that extend beyond the realms of orthodox Islam. Morocco's cultural past is rich and steeped within the systems of pre-Islamic beliefs of the Amazigh tribes, which preceded the arrival of the Romans, the Vandals, and Catholicism imported during the Spanish and French protectorates, all of which have left a veritable palimpsest of cultural practices that are to this day still thriving alongside the precepts of Sunni Islam. Thus, the practices of reciting a spell to ward off evil or jealousy, brandishing amulets and charms such as the *Hand of Fatima*, the visiting of seers, and the fear of *djinns* (wandering demons, the etymon of *genie*) are all very common among most Moroccans (Zwemer 125, 185).

For Moroccan writers and readers, the episode of the seer in Akalay's short story could follow the didactic nature of traditional Moroccan and Arabic literature and would not be as much of a novelty as it would be to the Western reader. It is here that we observe one facet of the hybridity of language found in Akalay, in which we find a Moroccan or orientalist version of *lo real maravilloso*, explained in the introduction of Alejo Carpentier's *El reino de este mundo*:

> [M]e dan ganas de repetir una frase que enorgullecía a los surrealistas de la primera hornada: *Vous qui ne voyez pas, pensez à ceux qui voient* [...]. Pero es que muchos se olvidan, con disfrazarse de magos a poco costo, que lo maravilloso comienza a serlo de manera inequívoca cuando surge de una inesperada alteración de la realidad (el milagro), de una revelación privilegiada de la realidad, de una iluminación inhabitual o singularmente favorecedora de la inadvertidas riquezas de la realidad, de una ampliación de las escalas y categorías de la realidad, percibidas con particular intensidad en virtud de una exaltación del espíritu que lo conduce a un modo de «estado límite». (3-4)

Be it in the forests of Haiti (in Carpentier's case), the home of a faithful Catholic in Buenos Aires, or in a home of a Moroccan village, there is a realm of miracles that can take place within reality, but faith, culture, and traditions can "amplify" scales and categories of reality as Carpentier explains. Between the East and West, this morphing of reality can work *both* ways and can distort and amaze the reader or the viewer in the moment of hybridity. Magical realism is an established tradition within the Latin American canon because of the cultural hybridity that thrives and has shaped Latin America. The weaving of the real with the fantastical is possible in Moroccan culture, a hybrid culture in its own right, even when Moroccan literature creates a hybrid or peripheral culture with (or within) the West through the Castilian language. It is always capable of expressing such magical realism as is present in "Casamiento frustrado." The Moroccan version of magical realism found in Akalay's story is a product of the hybridity of language and literary style, which brings into question the tensions between Orientalism and Occidentalism in modern Moroccan literature.

Through the act of writing in Castilian, a language bequeathed to a select few in the north of Morocco during the time of colonization, writers such as Akalay begin to occidentalize their writing, which is further developed through the use of Western literary style. They are adopting a language of the occidental "Other" in order to be understood, but, in order to be understood and remain engaging, writers such as Akalay risk self-orientalizing as Ricci has posited in his article, "Moroccan literature in Castilian," on borderland literature of Morocco (2007). I would also add that Moroccan magical realism in Castilian could contribute to self-orientalization, exclusively in the reception of a Western reader, as a Moroccan reader would probably identify with the biculturalism and hybridity of language and style of Akalay. This almost antithetical juxtaposition of social realism, a sort of journalistic testimony, with the fantastical has the ability to orientalize the characters. The way in which this juxtaposition is antithetical poses another problem: Is it in the gaze of every reader? It could be posited that a Moroccan reader would most likely not be taken aback when encountering this fusion of magical realism with journalistic realism as much as perhaps a Western reader in Spain. I believe, however, that this juxtaposition could offer a form of dialogue between Moroccan writers and Latin American writers who evidently share a similar tradition of magical realism. This commonality between Moroccan writers of Castilian expression and Latin American writers present a type of Orientalism not unlike that explained in Araceli Tinajero's *Orientalismo en el modernismo hispanoamericano* and Julia Kushigian's *Orientalism in the Hispanic Literary Tradition. In Dialogue with Borges, Paz, and Sarduy.*

Another form of hybridity of language and space within the tension of Orientalism and Occidentalism in Akalay's short stories emerge from the recurring themes of loss, death, poverty and the need to immigrate to Europe. Half of the short stories in *Entre Tánger y Larache,* including "Luz de vida," "El peso de la vida," "El peso del amor," "Promesas," and "Religión y valentía" are centered on the separation of man and woman, of a broken matrimony due to tragedy or widowhood. In "Luz de vida" we find a widower who has never progressed beyond the day of the death of his wife in spite of being surrounded by his daughter and his many grandchildren, at once a source of joy and despair for him. He is constricted within the confines of the bedroom he once shared with his wife. She is a specter that never seems to leave his side. He begs to her and he prays to her until she materializes into a vision:

> El anciano piensa intensamente en su amada, pero no como un pasado añorado, sino como una voz que oye muy cerca; que le susurra al oído palabras de ánimo: «vive tu vida; no te quedes anclado en la nada», oye que le dice la voz de su amada, muy quedo. Se echa en la cama y quiere sentirlo todo a través del corazón. Por un momento la ve frente a él, a los pies de la cama; no le dice adiós y sonríe. El hombre siente una extraordinaria ternura y cierra los ojos para que la visión permanezca dentro de él. (26)

Here again we find the occurrence of a vision within Akalay's narrative where the *negative* presence of the deceased goes beyond the realm of memory and into a metaphysical presence in the life of the widow or widower. The dead spouse is almost deified in the world of the widowed as one reads in "Promesas"; the newly widowed Ilhâm has to make the choice of leaving behind her young son with her mother and she must cross over clandestinely to Spain on the infamous and dangerous journey across the Strait of Gibraltar by raft. Throughout the narrative of her story she weaves a succession of prayers to Allah and to her husband for guidance and support and to justify herself for what she is doing:

> [E]stoy obligada a buscar fortuna a España. ¡Dios Todopoderoso, déjame que pruebe mi suerte en este país! Conozco su lengua y su gente; deseo trabajar para poder respetar la memoria de mi querido e inolvidable marido. ¡Ayúdame, Dios mío! Si él se ha ido, me toca a mí educar nuestro hijo; permíteme, Dios mío, alcanzar este objetivo. (48)

> Querido mío, tú sabes que no puedo hacer otra cosa. Mi situación en Marruecos se había hecho insoportable; sin trabajo y con nuestro hijo bajo mi responsabilidad [...] Ahora estoy en España y lo que he sufrido hasta el momento creo que merece la pena. No te preocupes por nada, que yo me las arreglaré y encontraré trabajo.... (52)

Between the harsh reality of her daily life as a single, widowed mother in Morocco, she finds solace in the spiritual realm of her life, of which Allah and her husband are still very much a part and over which they can still have influence.

Ilhâm undergoes a metamorphosis throughout the narrative in spite of her prayers. She explains that she has what it takes to assimilate into Spanish culture, as she already knows "su lengua y su gente." As she gets off the raft, she takes off her old Moroccan clothes and dons the appearance of a Western woman: a brand new dress, new high-heeled pumps, make-up, and red lipstick. Her cultural marginality as a bilingual Moroccan allows her to alter her appearance as soon as she touches Spanish soil: "¡Venga, a vestirse! Me pongo mi bonito vestido; mis zapatos nuevos que me compré para la occasion y este jersey para guardarme del frío; ¡tengo que estar bien guapa para que no sospechen!" (51). Ilhâm knows how she must appear in the eyes of Spaniards in order to avoid looking like a "clandestina" (51).

Here she is equating beauty with what, in Lugones' terms, would be a kind of Spanish "purity" that would allow her to fit in. Her cultural cross-dressing is a physical manifestation of the ease with which she slides from one margin of her identity to the other; she "curdles" or mixes her Moroccaness with her Spanishness. Each element has the capacity to hide the other. Though, for Ilhâm, the gaze of the Westerner has more weight in terms of her aesthetics. To be seen as Moroccan would negate her being "guapa." With her fluency in the Castilian language, she hopes to find employment quickly, which she does after a close "friend" implicates her in a Madrid-based prostitution ring, a reality that is all too common for many young North African women who arrive in Europe on their own with no system of support.

Within the system of hybrid space and language, Akalay, in his short story, "Religión y valentía," tries to find a moment of mediation and human commonality in spite of the ever-present tensions between Orientalism and Occidentalism in his literature and biculturalism, and confronts the question of Islam and its reception in the West. The post-9/11 world has left indelible memories of terror not only in the West, but also in the Islamic world. Akalay's self-critical eye would like the Castilian-speaking West to understand that North Africans are just as frightened by terrorists as any European or American. There is a reason for the existence of fanaticism, which is unfortunately born out of a tension between cultures in which people feel the need to defend their beliefs outside the limits of reason, thus contradicting their own morals.

"Religión y valentía" focuses on the separation of an elderly and pious Moroccan couple that together has formed a marriage that maintains the precepts of Islam as its foundation. The husband, appropriately named Mohamed, by Mohamed Akalay, dons a short beard and is a reader and reciter of the Qu'ran and very active in his local community. He and his wife are especially inspired by writings that demonstrate Islam as a peaceable faith and way of life. He reads the words of Abu Bakr, the first caliph of Islam, before going into battle:

> No traicionéis ni engañéis, no cometáis actos reprobables, ni mutiléis; no matéis a niños, ancianos, ni mujeres; no destruyáis ni dañéis las palmeras y tampoco las queméis. No cortéis árboles frutales, no degolléis corderos, vacas ni camellos. Pasaréis por pueblos que acostumbran a recluirse en sus conventos, invitados al Islam, pero no los obliguéis a retirarse de allí. ¡Partid! En el nombre de Dios. (72)

Mohamed holds steadfast to these words because he is aware of Western misperceptions of Islam as a bellicose faith. He repeats verses of the Qu'ran that demand that all Muslims be of moderate temperament and keepers of peace, community, and order. Akalay wants his Castilian-speaking readers in the West to find some commonality with the pious man, just as his counterpart in Madrid might recite prayers to Saint James and attend every Sunday mass without fail.

Mohamed, as an observant Muslim, must keep with all commandments, though he has never fulfilled one final pillar of Islam: the *Hajj*, or the pilgrimage to Mecca. As the couple lives by slender means, Mohamed decides to fulfill his *Hajj* on his own, much to his wife's chagrin, who prays and waits for him during the entire trip. Akalay changes the direction of the story quite abruptly and leaves the reader wondering if Mohamed ever made it to Mecca, as he is arrested en route before ever making *Hajj*:

> La policía llega rápidamente al lugar y detiene a varias personas, entre ellas a Mohamed, como uno de los presuntos causantes del hecho inhumano. Lo llevan a la cárcel y empiezan a interrogarle. Después de dos semanas de tortura y agresividad, lo entregan a otro país occidental y lo meten otra vez en la cárcel, donde permanece sin conocer la causa de su detención. Aquí conoce todas las for-

mas de torturas y castigos. (74)

Here, Akalay makes the West confront itself. Mohamed is mistaken for a terrorist after an attempted terrorist attack near his hotel. He – being Moroccan, a Muslim, and bearded man – clearly fits the description of a terrorist according to the Western gaze. Akalay puts his Western reader in a precarious situation as he writes in Castilian, which has enabled him to share Mohamed's life and spiritual intimacy with the reader in the reader's own language, not Arabic or a translation of Arabic. The Western reader is confronted with his or her own opinions of Islam at this moment of blatant injustice done through what can only be seen as a sort of "Western fanaticism" of protecting itself from the Other and at all costs. For the Moroccan reader living within the same space and peripheral culture as Akalay, this is a moment of *justice*: to have Westerners finally realize their own misconceptions of Islam.

Akalay goes further during this moment of confrontation between the West and Islam, and he uncovers the pivotal moment in which fanaticism is born with a person, here being the once-peaceable Mohamed after a protracted period of torture and abuse at the mercy of a Western prison:

> Ya es otro hombre, nervioso, indiscreto y charlatán; parece loco con sus nuevas ideas. Este extraño comportamiento conduce a la persona a la destrucción y al terror y crece en su mente la posibilidad de odiar a todos, sintiendo una sensación salvaje de venganza. La primera educación de tolerancia, convivencia y fraternidad se cambia por otra intolerante y fanática. (75)

Through the abuse he has suffered, Mohamed is now depicted as the failed Muslim, the fanatic, who will now defend himself by any means, including going against his own principal morals ("primera educación"). Akalay explains that there are "new ideas" in Mohamed's mind, which are born out of conflict and violence, not even leaving the shadow of who had once been the man. Though Mohamed returns home thanks to the benevolence of a French prison guard and a Christian couple, he is never quite the same. Westerners have been overly exposed to the concept of fanatical Islam after the wake of 9/11, but how does a "fanatical Western-culture" appear to Muslims and the rest of the East? Was not 9/11 a collective trauma that has left the West with its own "new ideas" not unlike those of Mohamed in prison? One is faced with the question regarding Moroccan immigrants and their remaining "culturally" Muslim. Are they forced to leave these parts of their identity behind? Does the West force "cultural" individuals to be "post-cultural," thus rendering them effaced of all traces that signal them as Other? Moreover, how is a Moroccan writer, such as Akalay, able to confront the West in order to present the "mirror" of fanatical cultures? It is only through the use of language, the language of the Western/Castilian Other, and the context of the hybrid space within Moroccan peripheral culture in the West that Moroccan writers can capitalize on their position as borderland writers and cultural mediators. Cultural mediation occurs in the presence of a bicultural—"curdled" in Lugones' terms—individual, such as Akalay, who has the agency to define his identity through his language and writing.

Moroccan writers have been left with the linguistic vestiges of a colonial past, thus it is no wonder that one can now find a variety of Moroccan literature in Castilian, French, Arabic, English, and Darija. Writers such as Akalay, who more than likely could have written in French or Arabic just as well, take great risks in publishing in Castilian, though they do so in the hopes of encouraging a form of cultural mediation and intercultural understanding between East and West, between European and immigrants, and even between the tensions within the multicultural Self that battles inwardly for a sense of belonging, acceptance and purpose. Lugones' theories of cultural "purity" and bicultural "curdling" offer an explanation as to how writers such as Mohamed Akalay are comfortable in mixing literary traditions as his writing is an extension of his identity of a Spanish-speaking and Spanish-educated Moroccan. He is breaking barriers that have been established through decades of nationalism and the establishment of a "unified" national identity in both Spain and Morocco.

Akalay does not try to be quintessentially Spanish or Moroccan and this in and of itself can seem as an act of subversion to some of his readers who may not want to accept the "curdling" of Spain and Morocco into one. Thus, one could posit that Akalay is making both of the countries confront each other and their own selves at once, not unlike Cadalso did through his voice as Gazel. Spain throughout history has never has been purely "Spanish." Regional languages have been silenced. Jews and Muslims were constantly banished from the peninsula after the end of the fifteenth century. Likewise, Morocco is clearly not purely and singularly "Moroccan" as I have explained in the introduction. There are Moroccans of Amazigh, Arab and Andalusian heritages. These communities live alongside one another and have mixed for centuries, but still there is no singular form of Moroccaness to serve as a symbol of Moroccan nationalism. Yet, there is tension between Occidentalism and Orientalism in Akalay's work that seems to raise questions on "purity" of literary style and the "purity" of cultural identity of its characters and of Akalay himself. Is he too Moroccan to pierce the Spanish-language literary world or is he too occidental to reach out and connect to his Moroccan readers?

The peripheral culture inside the West, such as a Moroccan ghetto in Spain or an academic department of Spanish philology at a Moroccan university, can serve as a space in which a hybrid language and literature can flourish. One must go back to Ricci's concern for the current marketability of such literature and his suggestion for "new critical vision" of the "peripheral culture" which thrives in the margins of East and West, Orientalism and Occidentalism. I posit that Akalay's *Entre Tánger y Larache* could possibly one of the first of a hopefully enduring wave of new Castilian-language Moroccan literature that will not only position itself in the literary market, but also in the creation of a cross-cultural dialogue through the acknowledgement of a hybrid space and language by both Moroccan and Spaniard, East and West.

Bibliography

Akalay, Mohamed. *Entre Tánger y Larache*. Madrid: SIAL Ediciones, 2006. Print.

Bennett, Milton J. "Cultural Marginality: Identity Issues in Intercultural Training." *Education for the intercultural experience*. Ed. R. Michael Paige. Yarmouth, ME: Intercultural Press, 1993. Print.

Bhabha, Homi. *The Location of Culture*. New York: Routledge, 1995. Print.

Cadalso, José. *Cartas marruecas; Noches lúgubres*. Ed. Joaquín Arce. Madrid: Ediciones Cátedra, 1995. Print.

Carpentier, Alejo. *El reino de este mundo*. New York: Edición Rayo, 2009. Print.

Flesler, Daniela. *The Return of the Moor: Spanish Responses to Contemporary Moroccan Immigration*. West Lafayette, IN: Purdue University Press, 2008. Print.

Kushigian, Julia. *Orientalism in the Hispanic Literary Tradition. In Dialogue with Borges, Paz, and Sarduy*. Albuquerque: University of New Mexico Press, 1991. Print.

Lugones, Maria. "Purity, Impurity, and Separation." *Signs: Journal of Women in Cultureand Society* 19.2 (1994): 458-479. Web.

Mernissi, Fatima. *Beyond the Veil: Male-Female Dynamics in Modern Muslim Society*. Bloomington, IN: Indiana University Press, 1987. Print.

Ricci, Cristián H. "African Voices in Contemporary Spain." *Hispanic Issues* 37 (2010): 203-231. Print.

—. "La literatura marroquí de expresión castellana en el marco de la *transmodernidad* y la hibridación poscolonialista." *Afro-Hispanic Review* 25.2 (2006): 89-107. Web.

—. *Literatura periférica en castellano y catalán: el caso marroquí*. Madrid: Ediciones del Orto, 2010. Print.

—. "Moroccan Literature in Castilian: Borderland Literature–Literature without Borders." *Alternative Orientalisms in Latin America and Beyond*. Ed. Ignacio López-Calvo. Cambridge: Cambridge Scholars Publishing, 2007. 192-204. Print.

—. Prólogo. *Entre Tánger y Larache*. By Mohamed Akalay. Madrid: SIAL Ediciones, 2006. Print.

Said, Edward. *Orientalism*. New York: Vintage Book, 1978. Print.

Tinajero, Araceli. *Orientalismo en el modernismo hispanoamericano*. West Lafayette, IN: Purdue University Press, 2004. Print.

Zwemer, Samuel. *Influence of Animism on Islam: An Account of Popular Superstitions*.Whitefish, MT: Kessinger Publishing, 2003. Print.

Costume, Couture, or Commerce?: Visions of Orientalism in María Dueñas' *El tiempo entre costuras*

Christina Vázquez Mauricio

Spain occupies a unique position amongst the former empires of Europe due to the fact that it was, for almost eight hundred years, a colonial possession and caliphate of the Arab empire. Julia Kushigian postulates that this has contributed to the country's relationship with its colonizer that is the contrary to other European colonial empires. Spain does not 'orientalize' the Arab world, but the opposite (2). Christians, Jews, and Arabs coexisted in such a way that almost all facets of Spanish culture today— the lexicon, language, architecture, music, and dance—exhibit the semblances of this period in the peninsula's history. The Spanish-Arabic relationship that has developed throughout centuries has been constant and specifically linked to the north of Africa, highlighted by the short thirteen kilometer distance that separates these two seemingly dissimilar worlds.

In recent history the relationship between Spain and northern Africa has been marred by problems of illegal immigration, drug trafficking, and differences regarding the status of the colonial territories Ceuta, Melilla, and Western Sahara. However, as of late there has been a certain interest to rediscover one particular time period within this history: the former Spanish Protectorate that existed from 1913 to 1958. The teaching of Spanish and other European methodologies in Moroccan schools, the rise and fall of Francisco Franco and his military formation in Africa, historical fiction novels, television series and movies based on real events are examples of the projects that have been incited by the history of Spain and the Protectorate.

This chapter will analyze the development of Orientalism throughout the pages of one such resurgence of interest in Spanish Morocco: María Dueñas' *El tiempo entre costuras* (2009), a novel that examines the Spanish-Arab relationship in the 1930s and 40s. The analysis will pay particular attention to the vision of Morocco in Spain, the vision of Spain in Morocco, and how tangible elements such as clothing and cultural artifacts are employed to illustrate Orientalism in a Spanish-Arab perspective. This work will also interweave a study of certain points of historical information where necessary to contextualize the world María Dueñas seeks to recreate through her characters.

"Orientalism" itself has many definitions, and many topics fall under its umbrella. According to Edward Said, Orientalism "derives from a particular closeness experienced between Britain and France and the Orient, which until the early nineteenth century had really meant only India and the Bible lands" (4), leading the English and French empires to adopt the role of 'protectors' of the countries they colonized. They theorized that simply being the 'Other' made them belong to a European "system of rule whose principle was simply to make sure that no Oriental was ever allowed to be independent and rule himself... since the Orientals were ignorant of self-government, [and] they had better be kept that way for their own good" (228). Julia Kushigian, whose theories will be further studied later on, deviates from Saidian Orientalism in regards to Spain. Although a former European colonizing superpower like England and France, Spain was, for almost eight centuries under the many Arab dynasties and caliphates that ruled the Iberian peninsula between 711 and 1492, the colonized, not the colonizer. Araceli Tinajero also differs radically from either of the aforementioned interpretations of Orientalism and postulates that there were cultural exchanges between subjects on the periphery, two "others" in the eyes of colonizing Europe. In her book *Orientalismo en el modernismo hispanoamericano*, she proposes that tangible cultural products from 'oriental' cultures present in both other 'oriental' and

'Western' societies enables a better understanding of the self through an in-depth analysis of the products' presence. Her theories will be employed later in this chapter as well.

It is alleged that the Protectorate was formed so that Spain could have annexed territories to serve as training grounds for the Spanish army; however, it should be noted that the inner-workings of the state and the rest of Europe were isolated from the quotidianlives of the individuals living in the territory. According to Susan Martin-Márquez in her book *Disorientations: Spanish Colonialism in Africa and the Performance of Identity,* it was Franco's goal that Spain would come to recognize a hereditary, sanguine relationship with Morocco that began much earlier than the creation of the Protectorate. Martin-Márquez, much like Kushigian, also parts from Edward Said's orientalist theories to postulate that Saidian theory does not answer for the unique relationship Spain has with the Arab world due to its position as one of this vast empire's colonized territories. However, she is in agreement with Said in the sense that franquismo[37] recreated the colonial philosophy that Europe was the benevolent colonizer, with "Spain imaged as playing the role of older and wise brother to the developmentally delayed younger African siblings… who better to raise an orphaned child than an elder member of his or her own family?" (Martin-Márquez 222). Notice the use of the phrase "developmentally delayed," whose definitions carry a negative connotation that can mean either an individual with cognitive deficiencies or something that is evolving at a rate slower than the norm and is thus behind. Martin-Márquez also cites Gil Benumeya who states that Spain and the north of Africa are "dos mitades de una fruta cortada en rodajas" (223). Again, Martin-Márquez's postulation is that Spain's relationship with Morocco is not only sanguine, but also that political ideologies during Franco's regime recreated a Saidian orientalist approach within Spain towards the north of Africa.

It is evident that the relationship between Spain and Morocco has been constructed throughout the years by the

---

37 A series of political ideologies linked to the regime of Francisco Franco (1939-1975).

Spanish government, yet it also seems to be a relationship that is present in the Spanish collective conscious. Rocío Velasco de Castro in her essay "La internacionalización del Protectorado de España en Marruecos" signals that Franco throughout his career attempted to design a type of international politics where long – and short-term projects were combined and employed to keep him in power. Morocco was a tool in this policy since it played a very important role in the projection of an anticommunist and catholic message to the rest of the world (163). The outbreak of World War I impelled a great number of expatriates to seek refuge in Tetouan, turning it into a cosmopolitan city in a relatively neutral territory, a reputation that it would maintain throughout the Spanish Civil War and World War II until the late 1950s. The Spanish and other Europeans in the Arab territory coexisted, at least superficially, in a way similar to the Arabs in al-Ándalus[38]. This chapter will analyze the interest taken in rediscovering this kinship in the context of *El tiempo entre costuras*, a novel that has in the last several years appeared in several bestseller lists, along with several texts that speak to the significance of the relationships that appear in the novel.

María Dueñas constructs an intricate and profound work of historical fiction that focuses on the events prior to World War II and their relationship with the Spanish Protectorate in Morocco. The novel weaves the story of Sira Quiroga, a young custom dressmaker from Madrid whose love for a wayward impresario drives her to embark on a trip to Tetouan that would change her life in a few short weeks after her arrival. Strapped by destiny and forced to live with a local matron, Sira discovers that through the precarious relationship she maintains with this woman, her dressmaking trade will become transformed into a simple façade for something much more complicated. Sira's story begins in early 1930s Madrid and the reader is transported throughout the course

---

38 Al-Ándalus describes the regions of the Iberian Peninsula governed by Muslims between 711 and 1492. This region's boundaries changed due to the outcomes of wars with Christian kingdoms and changes in caliphate dynasties.

of the novel to Tangiers and Tetouan in Morocco, a Nazi-sympathizing, postwar Madrid, and a cosmopolitan Lisbon that is colored by businessmen, refugees, and bohemians.

The novel opens with a description of the surroundings in which Sira grows up and works a typical Spanish environment of the early 20th century. The protagonist comes of age in a humble neighborhood away from the bustle of Madrid, juxtaposed against her working environment: doña Manuela's sophisticated atelier repudiated throughout Madrid thanks to the couture that dressed the modern women of the capital city. It is in that locale where Sira learns the skills that will later ensure her success when she finds herself exiled in the Protectorate (1913-1956). As tensions rise between loyalists of the Spanish crown and republicans, the Second Republic rises (1931-1939) and fewer clients enter and fewer dresses leave the atelier, foreshadowing what would happen in 1939. As mentioned earlier, the text remains quite faithful to history. Sira remains loyal to her fiancé Ignacio, a government employee with few ambitions, until she replaces him with Ramiro, a smooth-talking typewriter salesman. This fortuitous encounter leads Sira to abandon Madrid in the months leading up to the military uprising that would ignite the Spanish Civil War in 1936, dragged towards an uncertain future by the passion she feels towards a man she barely knows.

There is no mention of Morocco until Sira forges a romantic relationship with Ramiro and she is later convinced to leave Spain to open a branch of *Academias Pitman*, a technical academy that specialized in teaching necessary skills for the workplace, in Morocco. Upon recovering part of the unbeknownst inheritance her father leaves her, Ramiro attempts to persuade her to leave for Tangiers together. "Pero, ¿para qué van a querer los moros aprender a escribir a máquina?" (48), asks Sira upon hearing Ramiro's novel idea. Here one does not encounter an Orientalism of respect, as Kushigian would postulate, but a more Saidian approach that takes into account a possible stereotype. Sira speaks of the Moors in somewhat of a pejorative way, as if the Moors had no need to learn how to type because of their lack of intelligence. At times throughout the novel there are instances where, although the characters attempt to take a benevolent and respectful approach, there is evidence of stereotyping and lack of knowledge of the supposed 'other.' To Sira's question, Ramiro responds:

> Nuestra academia estará destinada a la población europea que vive en Marruecos: Tánger es una ciudad internacional, un puerto franco con ciudadanos llegados de toda Europa. Hay muchas empresas extranjeras, legaciones diplomáticas, bancos y negocios financieros de todo tipo... en Tetuán la situación es distinta... la población es menos internacional porque la ciudad es la capital del Protectorado español....(48)

Historically, the Morocco Conference (or the Treaty of Algiers, 1912) divided Morocco in two: a French zone and a Spanish zone, and simultaneously declared Tangier an international zone. The Spanish zone was the more problematic of the two due to the uninhabited Rif Mountains and Franco's later use of this territory as an instrument of his fascist propaganda (Sayahi 198). This section of land cut out for Spain in the treaty would be the Protectorate, much how Sira describes it: "después de firmar con Francia el Tratado de Algeciras por el que, como suele pasar a los parientes pobres, frente a los franceses ricos a la patria hispana le había correspondido la peor parte del país... la más indeseable. La chuleta de África, le decían" (190).

The treaty's terms stipulated that Spain would come to possess the worst part of the African territory for being what Sira calls the "poor kinsman" of France. In a way, the protagonist becomes a spokesperson for the relationship between Spain and Morocco, a type of interlocutor who weaves her own interpretations of and commentary on current events into the official, handed-down account of the diplomatic relations. Historical facts that occurred in the Protectorate are colored by the protagonist's struggle to recover part of her identity lost throughout her youth. In this way, one could apply an Orientalist reading to *El tiempo entre costuras*. According to

Julia Kushigian in the introduction to her book *Orientalism in the Hispanic Literary Tradition*, Hispanic Orientalism

> seeks to approach the Orient, the Other, not in a spirit of confrontation, but rather what may appear to be a need to preserve one's own identity. It encourages an enhanced, original view of the self, through a process of leaving the familiar and the secure, in which the Other advances an emotional and intellectual detachment that leads to an awareness of the self. (12)

Kushigian's Orientalist view differs from that of Said in that she accounts for Spain's constant relationship with the Orient – in this case, a vast Muslim territory directly south of it that for several centuries was the occupier, not the occupied. Sira, through her role as interlocutor for history, exemplifies the critic's quest for the 'self.' However, she not only assumes that role by simply 'telling' the history, or being the history's voice. Sira acquires and embodies self-awareness precisely how Kushigian stipulates it – through a 'process', a series of journeys across the very borders disputed in historical backdrop.

Upon leaving Madrid, Sira recounts her mother's farewell: "presentía que [su] separación no duraría demasiado: como si África estuviera al alcance con tan sólo cruzar un par de calles" (53). This can be interpreted as slightly more than a daughter who feels that her mother will perpetually be – at least emotionally – 'across the street.' It can serve to illustrate that Morocco was a land that the average Spaniard knew little of without personal knowledge, that it was 'at reach', yet faraway. Dueñas treads a fine line between depicting the Spain-Morocco relationship as, on the one hand pure military interest where Morocco is possessed by Spain, and on the other hand a foreign land inhabited by individuals that dress differently and are not of the same faith. Dueñas is careful to not have Sira become the voice for a pejorative, Saidian Orientalism. Contrary to a typical representation of the 'other,' by means of imaginary trips or a description of what one thought the 'other' would be like, it is noteworthy that Dueñas, with the exception of a few instances, depicts a Morocco free from preconceived notions and pretexts through Sira as if she were living in a place familiar to her. Upon arriving in Tangiers, Sira finds herself in

> una ciudad extraña, deslumbrante, llena de color y contraste, donde los rostros oscuros de los árabes con sus chilabas y turbantes se mezclaban con europeos establecidos... con su mar, doce banderas internacionales y aquella vegetación intensa de palmeras y eucaliptos; con callejuelas morunas y nuevas avenidas recorridas por suntuosos automóviles significados con las letras *corps diplomatique*... donde los minaretes de las mezquitas y el olor de las especias convivían sin tensión con los consulados. (53)

The Morocco Sira is coming to know is quite different from the Madrid she leaves behind. A strange yet brilliant city, the many different people living in Tangiers coexist with each other much like the smell of the spices coexist with the harshness of the consulate buildings. However, her time in this international city is abruptly cut short a few weeks after her arrival, when it emerges that she is another victim of Ramiro's frauds. He leaves her alone, pregnant, and responsible to pay the bill at the Continental Hotel where they stayed since their arrival in Tangiers. In a short note, Ramiro bids Sira farewell, saying that he has taken her father's inheritance money, promises to pay it back, and that it may behoove her to leave Tangiers as tensions rise. Sira takes a taxi to the bus station in an attempt to leave Tangiers but eventually faints from a miscarriage; she wakes up handcuffed to a hospital bed in Tetouan, in the Spanish Protectorate. The police chief informs her, among other things that she will have to repay the debt at the Continental hotel and move in to Candelaria's home, a matron who boards people in transit. There she will begin the two careers that will save her: a seamstress and a secret agent.

For Sira's first mission, Candelaria proposes smuggling a large number of guns to a point along the railroad by tying them to Sira's body with a series of bandages and then covering herself in a haik. This way, Sira easily passes for a Moor and does not raise the suspicions of any passersby. It is interesting to note the language Sira employs to describe her perception of the haik's construction and many functions:

> a diario veía a las mujeres árabes arrebujadas dentro de aquellas prendas anchas sin forma, esa especie de capas amplísimas que cubrían la cabeza, los brazos y el cuerpo entero por delante y por detrás. Debajo de ellas, efectivamente, podría alguien ocultar lo que quisiera. (118)

There are several orientalist interpretations that one could make in regards to the lexicon used to describe this article of clothing. The narration suggests that the haik is clothing without style or taste, and the women who wear it are wrapped up beneath "wide clothing without any shape" (118). This could be interpreted as a reverse-Orientalism; that is, a metaphor for the baseless cultural stereotype that Arabs have the reputation of hiding things such as the truth or 'not telling the whole story.' However, a deeper reading into Sira's simple act of putting on the haik can signify that the only visible separation between the Spanish women and the Moorish women living in the Protectorate was the layers of the haik's cloth; that is, behind the fabric, they were quite similar. This theory is furthered by Candelaria's comment upon seeing Sira dressed: "Perfecta, una morita más" (119). Thanks to this appearance, Sira could outwardly appear to be a Moor and not raise any suspicions about the guns strapped to her body.

She again employs the 'disguise' tactic when she is sent to Lisbon to earn the trust of Manuel da Silva, a textile entrepreneur from Portugal. Although she also does so as part of her work for the SOE[39], it is evident that she is comfortable playing the role of a Moorish woman. Through a conversation at the hotel where they meet for the first time, da Silva confesses that he has never been in Morocco despite having travelled around the world. Sira[40] responds:

> Es un país fascinante de gente maravillosa, pero me temo que le sería difícil encontrar allí mujeres como yo. Soy una marroquí atípica porque mi madre es española. No soy musulmana y mi lengua materna no es el árabe, sino el español. Pero adoro Marruecos: allí, además, vive mi familia y allí tengo mi casa y mis amigos. Aunque ahora resida en Madrid. (502).

Soon after the explanation of her origin, da Silva begins to speak of his silk-trading business and his dealings with Macau and China; his 'confession' that he has never been in Morocco could serve to highlight how the Portuguese man (and unofficially, Portugal) has had more contact with the countries of the Far East, and not Morocco. The relationship Arish forges with da Silva is purely commercial; this businessman's fabrics will eventually take with them invaluable messages sewn into their many rolls similar to Chez Arish's sewing patterns.

Sira's success as a seamstress pushes her and Candelaria to open an atelier in central Tetouan. Fustigated by the need to survive in her new home, the need to hide unmentionable truths about her past and some new precarious acquaintances, Sira forges an identity as the owner of a selective atelier. She describes herself as a

candidata incipiente a funcionaria... amante trota-

---

39 Special Operations Executive, created by Winston Churchill during World War II as an espionage and reconnaissance agency in territories occupied by the Axis powers.
40 At this point in the narration, she has come to be called "Arish." An explanation as to the change in her name is explained later.

mundos de un sinvergüenza... madre frustrada de un hijo nonato, sospechosa de robo cargada de deudas hasta las cejas u ocasional traficante de armas camuflada bajo la inocente nativa. En menos tiempo aún debería hacerme con una nueva personalidad porque ninguna de las anteriores me servía ya. (144)

None of Sira's former 'identities' could help her get out of the situation she was now in. It was only appropriate that she adopt a new one as a way to survive in Tetouan, a city whose unfamiliar culture would eventually come to offer refuge. According to Kushigian, "the New World is a metaphor of utopia, which is also, according to Renaissance thought, a metaphor of the Orient. Logically connected, the interanimation of Oriental images provides a renovating link that promotes an open dialogue between Spain and Hispanic America" (Kushigian 6). Although Kushigian here cites how Oriental images can bridge Spain and Hispanic America, her theory can also be applied to Spain's relationship with Morocco and, on a greater scale, with the Arab world. The relationship between Oriental images and their placement in a Western context and Araceli Tinajero's thoughts on the subject will be examined later. Here the focus will be on the sense of 'utopia.' A place that is unfamiliar can often be considered a utopic paradise where one can begin anew, free from past troubles. As soon as the ports and points of entry into the peninsula close, Sira's workshop in Tetouan opens for business and she is able to begin repaying her debts. Note that Tetouan offers Sira refuge not only from Tangiers but also from a Spain plagued by Civil War. Although Tetouan does not become a utopia where she lives free and disconnected from her many issues, it does offer her a sense of relative peace that she would not experience were she to be living a fugitive of the law in Tangiers or in her native, war-torn Spain.

From that point forward, Sira's life is colored by the coming and going of hundreds of clients from faraway lands in her atelier. A few short years later, when Franco's victory seemed imminent, Sira finds herself "cansada, harta, agotada, exhausta y, sin embargo, dispuesta a empezar a sacar las uñas para pelear por salir de [su] ruina" (Dueñas 172). As the business continues to prosper, Candelaria sends Jamila, one of her guests, to help Sira in the shop. This young Moroccan woman does speak, although rarely gives her opinion even when asked. Thanks to Felix, a young man living in the building across from the atelier, Sira fully integrates herself into the extremely educated and cultured society living in the Protectorate, and under his tutelage Sira also begins to usurp from her "castellano castizo los vulgarismos y las expresiones coloquiales y [creyó] un nuevoestiloparaobtener un mayor aire de sofisticación" (192). Felix is also responsible for adding the *h* at the end of her name in *Chez Sirah*; another one of his touches to "dotar al taller de un mayor aroma internacional" (192). In this way, one does not observe a Saidian Orientalism, but the opposite; it is a Spaniard living in Morocco who must adapt herself in many ways to an 'orientalized' society in order to fully integrate herself into the culture, especially in relation to the language. However, although Morocco is 'oriental' to Sira, it has been 'Westernized' by both the French and Spanish. Note how Felix gives Sira's atelier a French-sounding name, not a Spanish one, because French is the language used in Tangiers, the more international city of the newly divided Morocco.

María Dueñas is able to create a sense of veracity in her protagonist's story by incorporating historical characters into Sira's narration, such as Rosalinda Fox, mistress of Juan Luis Beigbeder, the High Commissary of the Protectorate. Rosalinda not only introduces Sira to a high-level clientele, but she is also responsible for bringing Sira's mother from Madrid to the Protectorate to escape the Spanish Civil War. These new friendships tie Sira to a life where she is committed to hide something much more cunning and precarious than a few simple *haute-couture* transactions. Through her relationship with Rosalinda and the commander Beigbeder, Sira becomes involved in the dealings of the British government living in the Protectorate and in Spain, whose goal is to tie the peninsula to the Allied forces at the onset of World War II. In order to fully develop her role as an SOE spy, she returns to Nazi-occupied Madrid with a Moroccan passport. The narration changes abruptly when a woman named Arish Agoriuq enters the scene, a woman who is surrounded by the wives of the Reich's brass living in Madrid. These women supplanted to the Spanish capital visit the atelier of Arish Agoriuq – Sira Quiroga spelled backwards – in order to enjoy the marvels this 'Arab' seamstress has brought from the Protectorate. Through Agoriuq's eyes, the reader enters into a realm of espionage that will dictate the progression of the rest of the novel.

It is interesting to note the instances of Orientalism once the narration takes the reader back to Nazi-occupied Madrid. Arish's purpose was to work as a seamstress in the same way she had done in Tetouan, only this time under the name "Arish Agoriuq." With this new name, she would forge her identity as a reputable Moroccan seamstress in Nazi Madrid who, due to a lack of quality textiles in Spain, would start an atelier with the purpose of incorporating Moroccan styles and fabrics into her designs. "No era un nombre árabe en absoluto," narrates Sira when recounting the origin of her new name, "pero sonaba extraño y no resultaría sospechoso en Madrid, donde nadie tenía idea de cómo se llamaba la gente allá por la tierra mora, allá por tierra africana, como cantaba el pasodoble" (378). Once more, there is evidence of Orientalism. Sira adopts a new name that, to unknowing Spaniards that knew next to nothing about life in Morocco, sounded exotic and therefore would not raise any suspicions. It is worth mentioning that it is those who live in the Protectorate who are able to adapt to two ways of life, who can relate to two different cultures and who are aware of what is going on in both Spain and Morocco, not those who are living in the capital. With this new identity, Arish has to compile information about the social agenda of Nazi officials living in Madrid—their every move, the parties they organize and the reason for organizing them, etc.—through conversations with their wives, lovers, and daughters that frequent the atelier in order to leave dressed in the most modern clothing. Arish later complies this data, translates it into Morse code, and inscribes it very carefully into sewing patterns so that they may pass into the right hands without raising suspicions.

In order to fully incorporate herself into these conversations and develop her work as a spy, Arish requires the help of two sisters, former helpers in the house of Beigbeder who speak Spanish as perfectly as they do German. Once more, evidence of Orientalism: now that a significant number of Nazis have moved to Madrid—that is, the city has become 'orientalized'—speaking Spanish alone is no longer enough. It is interesting to note that when Sira was in Morocco, Spanish was one of many languages spoken and she did not require anyone's help as an interpreter; however, Arish (Sira, in reality) requires the help of others to do her job in Spain. This is an example of Saidian Orientalism and is in the same vein, although on a much smaller scale, as the situation in India upon the arrival of the British. India's many languages fragmented the country were of no use to the Crown, so it became necessary for all to learn English so as to assuage any possible communication issues. While Spanish was still the primary language spoken in the country as a whole, German was the language spoken amongst the most powerful families in Madrid at that time, that is, within her atelier.

The importing of many Moorish products to decorate the atelier constitutes one of the most powerful instances of Orientalism present in *El tiempo entre costuras*. It was necessary to adapt to this new identity in as many ways possible, albeit externally, to give the atelier an authentic Moroccan appearance. As Kushigian argues, there is "a spirit of veneration and respect" towards the Orient in Spain that is not seen in any other European country; moreover, this type of Orientalism attempts to open an exchange between both cultures in order to learn about the self through the other (3).

However, in order to more thoroughly understand the importance of importing and exhibiting oriental products in the West (in this instance, Moroccan products in Spain), one must give special attention to the theory exposed in Tinajero's work titled *Orientalismo en el modernismo hispanoamericano*. In the third chapter of her book, she postulates that 'real' experiences are contextualized by contact with certain cultural products and artifacts, and that those experiences with tangible items promote a deeper understanding of the self. By crossing borders, these products and their later representation in written texts allow both the characters in the text as well as the reader "cuestionar y apreciar el arte y la estética desde una cultura 'periférica' hacia otra 'periférica'" (71). Sira feels comfortable playing the role of Arish in Madrid; although she became accustomed to the Moroccan way of life in Tangiers, she adopts and assumes the role of Arish in such a way that she, her atelier included, feels protected by her new identity and outward image. Arish buys

> un buen número de revistas y algunas piezas de artesanía marroquí con la ilusión de dar a [su] taller madrileño un aire exótico en concordancia con [su] nuevo nombre y [su] supuesto pasado de prestigiosa modista tangerina... las paredes pintadas en blanco satinado, la tarima de roble del suelo recién pulida.... (405)

Tinajero's theory, although written to question Edward Said's one-sided vision of Europe's Westernized colonies and the experience of non-European countries in light of his theory, can also be applied to the experience of some European countries, particularly Spain. About the contact with Oriental products, Tinajero states that such a contact and its depiction in writing "es la que permite a ese publico valorar también desde su propia sensibilidad, la estética oriental dentro de su contexto. Al atravesar tales fronteras, el texto nos permite conocer una nueva dimensión que une a dos culturas no europeas" (71). Again, the theory of two cultures that can come to know each other can also apply to a European culture coming into contact with a non-European culture. Note how Sira also teaches Marina, one of the young assistants, how to prepare tea

> a la manera moruna, con la hierbabuena que plantamos en macetas de barro sobre el alféizar de la ventana de la cocina... hasta le enseñé a pintarse los ojos de khol y cosí a su medida un caftán de raso gardenia para dar a su presencia un aire exótico. Una doble de mi Jamila en otra tierra, para que la tuviese siempre presente. (409)

In the case of the Moroccan products brought to Arish's atelier in Madrid and the preparation of tea, Tinajero's theory also applies. She states that "un artifacto cultural, sus relaciones, sus contextos, su vitalidad, funciones y asociaciones, concretamente existen mientras éste simultáneamente participa en un espacio discursivo y textual" (Tinajero 72) and therefore, the tangible item takes on a role more significant than just, for example, a Moroccan magazine or tea. Although at first glance, it could be argued that Sira adopts Arish's Moroccan identity in order to not raise suspicions, in this instance one can see that the protagonist employs cultural products and tangible elements to give the appearance of seeming exotic. She feels more comfortable in the role of a spy under her Moorish exterior than doing it in any way that would identify her as Spanish, and in order to do so comfortably, the protagonist brings in these products to give the workshop an air of authenticity.

An Orientalist approach to María Dueñas' *El tiempo entre costuras* could be based, much like what Kushigian postulates, on a continuous fusion and separation of the East and West in Spain in order to mix the two in a way that other countries could not (Kushigian 11). The lives of Sira Quiroga and Arish Agoriuq develop around this fusion of cultures and her double life as spy and seamstress, all under the constant threat of a Nazi invasion in England and the constant memory of her native Madrid while she lives in Tetouan. The protagonist shows her capacity for adapting to change by means of a chameleonic transformation into different characters that is conditioned by the needs her surroundings.

In an article written in *Panorama Audiovisual* to announce the end of the filming of a television series based on this novel, María Dueñas characterizes her book as one that has a "ritmo imparable cargada de encuentros y desencuentros, de identidades encubiertas y quiebros inesperados; de ternura, traiciones y ángeles caídos." Throughout the more than 600 pages, the colors, sounds, textures, and aromas of interwar Spanish Morocco are fused with the lives and comings and goings of the expatriates that the protagonist comes to meet thanks to her work in the atelier. The author manages to paint a panorama of the Arab world that is uniquely Spanish and does so, for the most part, with delicacy, respect, and admiration in addition to providing us with historical information. The author also clues the reader in to the fact that there were laws that protected Moroccans living under Spanish rule, increasing the awareness of both cultures. For example, when Sira attempts to execute her gun contraband, she hears by chance a conversation between two guardsmen in the public bathroom where one says to the other "como el sargento se entere de que has andado molestando a una marroquí libre de sospecha, te vas a comer tres días como tres soles de arresto en la Alcazaba, chaval" (133).

Does the widespread success of this work truly show that there is currently resurgence in interest in this topic? Does an orientalist approach to Dueñas' work, or other works similar to it, enable Spaniards to understand themselves deeper, in light of their relationship with Morocco? Despite the many facets of the unique Spain-Morocco relationship depicted in Dueñas' novel, it by no means is the only work in this vein. As mentioned earlier, other projects have been done and others are currently underway that center on this subject. Television shows like the one based on this novel or others such as *Amar en tiempos revueltos* or *Toledo*, as well as documentaries that examine the current relationship like *Españoles en el mundo: Marruecos*, deserve as much attention as *El tiempo entre costuras*. It is clear that not one Orientalist vision operates as a catchall; different elements of each of Said, Kushigian, Martin-Márquez, and Tinajero's theories apply to the unique Spain-Morocco relationship. An analysis of this novel is a mere grain of sand. In order to understand the revival of this history and just how deeply rooted is this interest in doing so, the other media that have surfaced need equal consideration.

Although Sira Quiroga and Arish Agoriuq move in two very different words— poverty and luxury, cosmopolitan Africa and interwar Spain, lackluster desert towns and majestic European embassies—there is another aspect of this novel that comes to light. María Dueñas weaves an audiovisual plot that is both lived and felt by the reader, and it is done so credulously, without any faults in the plot. Parts of the novel are pure narration and others develop as if they were meant for the theater, but it is done in its entirety with a precise and well-researched historical background.[41] It is true that the plot is based on the various relationships forged by the seamstress, but this cast of both real and fictional characters give authenticity to what *El tiempo entre costuras* sets out to do: to weave the story of the unique Spanish-Moroccan relationship during the time of Franco, in a credible way that is attainable by all types of audiences.

BIBLIOGRAPHY

Alcaraz Cánovas, Ignacio. *El Protectorado de España en Marruecos y el Frente Popular. Centro de Investigación y Estudios Republicanos*, n.d. Web. 10 Mar. 2012.

Amar en tiempos revueltos: Temporada 7, Episodio 1. RTVE, 5 Sept. 2011. Web. 14 Mar. 2012.

Así es 'El tiempo entre costuras'. Antena 3 TV, 7 Sept. 2011. Web. 12 Mar. 2012.

Dueñas, María. *El tiempo entre costuras*. 2nd ed. New York: Atria Español, Simon & Schuster, 2011. Print.

El-Madkouri Maataoui, Mohamed. "España y el mundo árabe: Imagen e imaginario." *Revista Electrónica de Estudios Filológicos*. June 2004. Web. 11 Mar. 2012.

Españoles en el mundo: tercera parada: Sur de Marruecos. RTVE, 11 Mar. 2009. Web. 12 Mar. 2012.

'Españoles en el mundo' viaja a Marrakech, ciudad de zocos, artesanos y palacios. RTVE, 11 Feb. 2011. Web. 21 Mar. 2012.

---

41 See the official blog official for *El tiempo entre costuras*, where María Dueñas presents her historical research about her book: http://eltiempoentrecosturas.blogspot.comADD

Kushigian, Julia. *Orientalism in the Hispanic Literary Tradition. In Dialogue with Borges, Paz, and Sarduy.* Albuquerque: University of New Mexico Press, 1991. Print.

Macías, Fernando. *'Amar en tiempos revueltos' estrena su séptima temporada, con caras nuevas y antiguos vecinos.* RTVE, 24 Aug. 2011. Web. 14 Mar. 2012.

"María Dueñas afirma que no le importa la etiqueta de escritora de 'best sellers'". QUE.es, n.d. Web. 7 Mar. 2012.

Martin-Márquez, Susan. *Disorientations: Spanish Colonialism in Africa and the Performance of Identity.* New Haven, CT: Yale University Press, 2008. Print.

"Boomerang TV finaliza el rodaje de 'El tiempo entre costuras' para Antena 3," *Panorama Audiovisual*, **2011, Panorama Audiovisual, S.A.,** 11 February 2012.

Ryan, Michael. *Teoría literaria: Una introducción práctica.* Trans. Francisco Martinez Osés. Madrid: Alianza Editorial, 2002. Print.

Said, Edward. *Orientalism.* New York, NY: Vintage Books: Random House, 1979. Print.

Sayahi, Lotfi. "El español en el norte de Marruecos: historia y análisis." *Hispanic Research Journal* 6.3 Oct. (2005): 195-207.*JSTOR.* Web. 10 Mar. 2012.

Tinajero, Araceli. *Orientalismo en el modernismo hispanoamericano.* West Lafayette, IN: Purdue University Press, 2004. Print.

Toledo, una serie histórica a la vez que contemporánea. Antena 3 TV, 12 Jan. 2012. Web. 13 Mar. 2012.

Velasco de Castro, Rocío. "La internacionalización del Protectorado de España en Marruecos: Reivindicaciones nacionalistas y aspiraciones españolas en el marco de la posguerra mundial." *Norba: Revista de Historia* 20 (2007): 161-72. *Universia.* Web. 10 Mar. 2012.

Part three:

Transpacific orientalisms

Mario Bellatín: Ghosts, the Human Body, and the Spaces Where They Meet

Kathryn Mendez

Mario Bellatín's novels start immediately in a state of delirium. There is usually one main character that is subject to this state, and the writer's style brings his readers right into the middle of the protagonist's thought process. There is often considerable separation between the protagonist and the narrator; while the narrator is often someone who is participating in the overall story, they are observing in an uncannily omniscient way the dreams and hallucinations of the novel's protagonists and those of the ones who are close to them. Here I would like to discuss two recent novels by Mario Bellatín, connecting them with two of his older and more critically studied novels: *La clase muerta* (2011), *Disecado* (2011), *El jardín de la señora Murakami* (2000), and *Shiki Nagaoka: Una naríz de ficción* (2001). While there has already been much written about the earlier novels, it is useful to revisit them when exploring the newer publications because there are themes and ideas that are constantly revisited throughout the spectrum of Bellatín's work as well as cultural themes and stylistic influences from other writers that can be fleshed out by noting both recent and older texts and criticism. Each one of the four novels by the author insists upon the participation of the reader in exploring the use of Japanese vocabulary and explanation of cultural customs that may or may not be fictional. The author has openly admitted to creating his own glossaries and terminology without researching them, but rather by adding them to his work as part of his artistic signature. Many of his novels also rely heavily on the use of photography as a way of mocking reality, and they are loaded with autobiographical references about the author himself. There is constant mention of ghosts, doppelgangers, and asexualized, deformed bodies and the enclosed spaces where they dwell, leaving the reader to feel a certain madness upon completing one (or several) of this author's semi-autobiographies. Like Borges, Bellatín does not tell his readers how to interpret his work, but rather he suggests many possibilities and leaves much of the work and exploration to the reader. María Rosa Menocal writes that Borges plays this same game of hiding truths within his texts: "Death and memory and the apparent vanity of doing much about either: death comes and memory, just as inexorably, slips away, except of course... through the magical powers of poetry, of writing. Borges has tricked us, with too obvious names and story lines..." (109). I would say that Mario Bellatín shows the exact same behavior in his writing style by hiding complex thoughts about the nature of what it means to be imperfectly human within what might appear to be a simple story of a frustrated, sad woman or an ill, deformed man. It is interesting also that both Borges and Bellatín draw from other cultures, particularly Asian and American Indian cultures, in order to explore these types of difficult questions that do not have answers (such as "What is truth?" or "What/whom should we believe?"). Perhaps this exploration of other cultures helps broaden the possibilities of what (im)mortality means, and what is its place might be within the dimensions of time and the act of writing.

For the purposes of studying Orientalism, Bellatín is an excellent example of a modern orientalist author because he often writes about Asian characters (mostly Japanese) by using examples of their language, customs, clothing and physical attributes, yet he constantly removes them from a completely Asian context first, by writing his books in Spanish, but also by making references to Western countries such as Germany, the United States, Mexico and Brazil. An excellent example of this modern orientalism is *El jardín de la señora Murakami* because it is a book written in Spanish about a woman torn between the ambitions and styles of western culture and the pressures of tradition and family values of Japanese culture. While at all times using the image of the garden as a mirror for her emotional state or for foreshadowing events, this character,

Izu—who as a married woman loses her identity and becomes simply la Señora Murakami—finds bitterness and shame in aspects of both of these cultures, resulting in the creation of a character that appears to be driven by simple motives but is actually quite complex and connected to both traditional female imagery from Japan as well as popular cult images in Latin America. According to Julia A. Kushigian, "Hispanic Orientalism comprises a generosity toward, and respect for, diversity" (3). This novelist falls gracefully into Kushigian's description of a Hispanic orientalist who prefers to participate in (and not simply represent) the cultures of the Orient by placing himself there while not getting too wrapped up in his own origin or place of residence. In fact, there is never any concrete indication of where the majority of the protagonists reside, and although often it appears to be in an unnamed land that strongly resembles Japan, sometimes the writer also hints that it is not. While Bellatín basically describes his characters as being Japanese, he often situates them in a space where Japan is part of a character's memory and not necessarily their place of residence. In most cases, for the novels discussed in this chapter, "Bellatín sets his novels on an unnamed island (but) he leaves an indelible Japanese imprint on his protagonists" (Donoso Macaya 132). Occasionally we are "oriented" in Sao Paulo, Brazil, for example, or we are told that a certain relative or acquaintance has gone to San Francisco in the United States, but this constant disorientation of the protagonists and the readers is methodical and purposefully used to bring the reader closer to the author's intentions of questioning reality. There are many references to relationships between Germany and Japan in particular, and in *El jardín de la señora Murakami* the author actually makes references to moments when protagonists have traveled to Germany or lived in Japan, but these references to geographic stability constantly appear to be in the past with no specific reference to where his characters are rooted in the present. Again like Borges, Bellatín uses settings that appear to be rather normal and often drab to hide his tidbits of mystery and wonder, and part of this is by evading the question of where exactly the protagonists are living, while at the same time skillfully presenting the question of whether some of them even exist at all.

Bellatín is not shy about sharing the autobiographical contributions to his novels. In an article from the compilation *La novela según los novelistas* (2007), the author explores an image that has followed him constantly since the writing of *Salón de belleza* (1994): "Peces atrapados en un acuario, suspendidos en un espacio artificial que poco tiene que ver con el entorno real en que la pecera está colocada.... pensando con terror en el riesgo que tiene cualquiera de quedar encerrado sin posibilidad de salida" ("Underwood Portátil. Modelo 1915" 159).With this openly stated fear, it is easy to look into the special circumstances of each of the protagonists and find the places where they are trapped like fish in a tank. In *El jardín de la señora Murakami*, the protagonist is constantly enclosed in gardens. While she ventures into the world outside of her gardens, she ultimately fails at her attempts to live in the outside world, and she becomes not only a silent body inside of a lavish garden, but also a rare piece in her husband's art collection, a collection that she initially criticizes for not being authentic but rather carelessly put together. And as a punishment, she becomes a wife and a statue in his garden, while her doppelganger, Etsuko, roams the unnamed city for hours without much explanation as to where she goes or why. This particular novel is most interesting because the protagonist is female (unlike the other novels discussed in this chapter), and I would venture to say that Izu is a sinister female character.

I also choose to use the word doppelganger for her servant Etsuko for a variety of reasons. First of all, there are several references made to Germany in more than one of Bellatín's novels. The word "doppelganger" means "double walker" in German and is considered a ghostly double of a living person with a sinister side. If Izu and Etsuko are both sinister women, then who is the actual doppelganger? There is never any certainty about this, nor is there any kind of resolution that indicates that the two women are the same person (in fact, the writer describes in detail their physical differences), yet their interactions with each other and with Señor Murakami might lead one to believe that Murakami was having an affair with Etsuko as he asks to see her breasts "one more time" in his moments of delirium before death, although there is never any proof that he had ever seen them in the first place. Any kind of indication that there is physical contact between Etsuko and/ or Izu and Señor Murakami is all speculation. The physical contact either happens in the imagination or in enclosed spaces that the reader can barely see, such as in the back seat of a car or in a hotel room where "supposedly" there is proof that sexual interactions occurred. But again, when Señor Murakami is dead, his ghost still appears in the garden where Señora Murakami passes her days, the same way that strange splashes of yellow (like Etsuko's yellow sweater) kept appearing in her parents' garden before her marriage and before she and Etsuko were to part ways definitively.

Interestingly enough, in Bellatín's novel *Shiki Nagaoka: Una nariz de ficción*, Etsuko is also the name of Shiki Nagaoka's sister, "a model of Japanese loyalty, kindness and sacrifice among siblings" (Tsurumi 144). It is interesting how these two novels, written within a year of one another, share the name of an important character that leaves questions about the role of the Japanese woman and about the author's intentions in portraying her. While perhaps the Etsuko of *Shiki Nagaoka* was in fact devoted to her brother until the end in spite of his being disowned by family, the Etsuko from *El jardín de la señora Murakami* in her role as doppelganger is quite different (despite her appearance of being a loyal servant), and my suggestion is that there are no innocent players here, especially not the female characters, particularly in *El jardín de la señora Murakami*.

Beyond suggesting that Izu (the future Señora Murakami) only appears to be an innocent victim in the world of Japanese culture and male predators, I would also suggest that Izu is the Japanese equivalent to Mexico's "La Pelona" or possibly a reflection of some of Latin America's other nearly mythical female figures. La Pelona, along with other Mexican female images, is a figure that has become a regular part of popular culture around the globe. It is the image of a skeleton lavishly dressed and often associated with the celebration of the Day of the Dead; she is not necessarily associated with fear, yet at the same time she is grotesque in her combination of beauty and horror. There are other female images in Mexico that bear this dual relationship such as "La Malinche", the legendary native American lover of Hernán Cortés who acted as his translator and guide during his conquest in Mexico and who is blamed for betraying her people by helping Cortés follow through with his destruction of the Aztec empire. Even Frida Kahlo in more recent decades has taken on a "mass-produced image (which) frequently enters the public sphere along with its confused mythology of pain and betrayal" (Friis 53). Incidentally, there is also a shared commonality between artists like Kahlo and Bellatín who focus their artistic efforts on failing bodies and the misery of living with physical (and emotional) pain. In all of the novels described in this chapter, the presence of physical pain or deformation is a main theme. Ronald J. Friis also mentions that "one key image shared by…Kahlo is an organic view of life in which subjects are tied to the earth and to each other by root systems" (55). Isn't Izu's relationship with her family's garden and later her relationship with her husband's garden the same thing? Bellatín, whether consciously or not, transfuses these American (and particularly Mexican) imageries into his Japanese characters. In other words, Izu, like la Malinche, is torn between two cultures and eventually participates in a betrayal of one culture for another in the incident where she exposes her progressive, westernized professor and shortly after accepts a traditional Japanese marriage agreement with Señor Murakami.

Like Frida Kahlo, Izu is rooted to her different phases of life through the presence of a garden and exposure to the effects of physical pain and death (and at the end of her husband's life she tries to uproot the bamboo from their garden), and like La Pelona, she is death disguised in a beautiful kimono who appears to be present at the death of nearly every man with whom she comes in contact. As Izu's father is dying, she, her mother, and Etsuko (doppelganger) all take turns in giving him massages for hours each day. Nothing seems to improve his situation, yet they continue to do so with eternal patience almost until the end of the novel. Diana Palaverisch describes this same kind of disconnected devotion to the sick in Bellatín's *Salon de Belleza* (1994): "La dedicación fría, efici-

ente y cruel por su desapego emotivo, convierte al protago-
nista en un santo singular, sin lágrimas ni compasión" (35).
This kind of emotionless compassion that Izu shows her father could be seen as "saintly" behavior, but upon reading
the novel again, it can turn into something darker depending
on how one approaches the text. Izu loses two fiancés before
her eventual marriage to Señor Murakami; one suitor is bitten
by a rabid dog after visiting her and he dies rather sudden-
ly; the other escapes to San Francisco never to be heard from
again. She is also present at Señor Murakami's death, and in
the overall picture there is no man left unscathed by her in this
book unless he escapes her or is attracted to other men and
therefore not apparently susceptible to Izu's power.

In the case of the dying father, his love for his daughter
was not a sexual love, and he still died in her presence; Izu
even had a baby brother she never met who also died apparently as a result of foreign bombings (again, a subtle use of
cultural hybridity). And once she is left alone to ponder the
ruins of her brush with humanity, strange things also start
happening in her gardens. One garden is kept in perpetual
winter for over a year, yet eventually summer does come with
a wave of heat and a loss of patience. Izu also tries to uproot
and destroy the lavish garden created for her by her husband
after his death, but she is unsuccessful. Could this be a way
of saying that while Death can have her way with man and
all its creations, at the end, the beauty of nature will endure
beyond her wrath? Even Bellatín says in his own article, "Underwood Portátil. Modelo 1915" that there are many relationships that can be established between beauty and death. The
author states: "...la belleza y la muerte deben ser las guías de
todo ser humano superior" (163). Beauty and death are two
things that also transcend time; from all of the hours of patience that Izu spent as a student and as a daughter, to all the
patience and waiting in her garden that were spent once she
was married, none of these seemed to affect the beauty of the
gardens nor the constant presence of death that surrounded
her on all sides. In some ways, she was enclosed by several
different walls—the walls of her gardens, the deaths and illnesses that surrounded her, the barriers of time and patience

that constantly restrained her—and she dealt with these walls by constructing several images of herself: Izu dressed in western-style school clothes, Izu in a kimono, Izu as Etsuko, and Señora Murakami as the ghost of Izu, enclosed inside the not very valuable collection of art displayed by her dead husband.

The critic Rebecca Riger Tsurumi has some very insightful thoughts on Izu and her role as a Japanese woman torn between progressive and traditional culture, yet in many ways I do not agree with her portrayal of the protagonist. It is suggested that Izu marries Murakami as an act of devotion towards her father (135), yet, as described above, I do not think it was an act of devotion to anyone or anything other than vengeance. The overly logical explanations for Izu's actions are accompanied by vague conclusions about the role of the garden as a "tool of hatred and vengeance" (140). On a deeper and perhaps more surreal level, I hypothesize that the author makes his protagonist's actions seem logical and ordinary for a woman of her circumstances and cultural mores, while really underneath she is a daft and vengeful woman who creates chaos everywhere she goes and dedicates her life patiently to vengeance. Tsurumi considers Bellatín's portrayal of women as "naïve...weak [and] subordinate" (149). In the case of *El jardín de la señora Murakami* I would absolutely disagree. Thinking back on the three examples of Mexican popular cultural imagery of women (La Pelona, La Malinche, Frida Kahlo), while these women on the outside have the reputation of being weak by death, or a traitor, or a victim of heartbreak and physical pain, it is actually these same women that have been responsible for tremendous cultural influence and, whether fictional or real, they have proven to follow motives of their own that were not completely controlled by the men with whom they associated or the cultural mores that bound them.

The suffering displayed by many of the male characters in *El jardín de la señora Murakami* is something that can be found in each of the other novels discussed in this chapter. In *Shiki Nagaoka: Una naríz de ficción*, the protagonist has a nose so large and painful that it impedes his ability to eat and he must use grotesque contraptions to express the pus from it on a regular basis. Just like for Izu's father, Bellatín takes pains to show the different procedures that one must endure when the body does not function as it should. It is noted that both in *Shiki Nagaoka* and *El jardín de la señora Murakami* the male characters act as negative forces, whether they are husbands, fathers, teachers, or suitors (Tsurumi 148). Many of these male characters, because of their illnesses or deformities, express the need to be in an enclosed space. Shiki Nagaoka encloses himself in a monastery, and when he is released from the monastery he becomes a recluse with no friends besides his sister.

The final book by Bellatín's *Shiki Nagaoka* written in a state of seclusion "deals with the relationship between writing and physical defects" (147), is an unmistakable allusion to the novelist's own relationship with writing as a possible remedy to deal with his own ill health. This suggests that perhaps Bellatín creates these characters so as to not have to confront such issues on a personal level; although the similarities of his characters with himself suggest autobiographical writing, the author is protected within a layer of fiction by turning aspects of himself into someone else in order to explore his own artistic psyche from an outside yet deeply personal point of view. In *Disecado*, the narrator is enclosed in his own room with a series of uncomfortable illnesses; in this case, the autobiographical touch of the author is impossible to ignore. The narrator finds Mario Bellatín (el ¿mi yo?) sitting at the side of his bed; a ghost, a doppelganger. The two men (or one man) share the sickness with his vision: "el autor fue contagiado por su propia creación" (*Disecado* 17) and the apparition questions the act of creation while at the same time lamenting the profound loneliness of living in a world with millions of people. The ¿mi yo? is always carrying a ghostly book, remembering the process of his own death, and having visions of a being with the face of a photograph of his grandmother and his dead dog. This novel is total ego masturbation. According to Ariés, Gorer, and Barthes, reading and mourning have both been compared to masturbation in a way that these are all examples of a self-focused, solitary activity that is deeply personal, seeking release from inner urges and turmoil that is incredibly difficult to explain with words. Ariés writes in his book *Western Attitudes Towards Death* (1974): "Like the sexual act, death was thought of as a transgression which tears man from his daily life, from rational society... plunging him into an irrational, violent and beautiful world" (57). While it is not usually a sound critical practice to link fiction with the autobiography of an author, it is difficult to avoid the sensation that Bellatín has written novel upon novel to explain his own inner disturbances, particularly because he is so open about including himself in photographic images in his works, and because of articles like "Underwood Portátil. Modelo 1915" (2007) in which he explains his own thoughts and point of view on his relationship to characters that appear to be his own doppelgangers: ill, deformed, enclosed.

Why can we call this "auto-fiction" (a term introduced by Ángeles Donoso Macaya) instead of autobiography? One could argue that the creation of any work of fiction is an author's own Frankenstein's monster; the characters become deformed mirror images of the author that take on lives of their own. It would not be fair to single out Bellatín's characters as subconscious versions of himself. Many of them are already dead or never existed. Donoso Macaya also makes the effort to point out that "Bellatín parece sugerir en estas narraciones que el gesto autobiográfico es, siempre, un gesto mentiroso, un gesto engañoso" (102). Yet it appears that for our author it is particularly difficult to escape the personal connection between beauty and death, and the obsessive and almost sexualized transfixion of his own story in each of these novels brings them a terrible beauty that is not common in other works. From an orientalist point of view, it is interesting how the theories of Ariés connect with Bellatín's obsession with Oriental cultures. Ariés notes how it is becoming more and more common in the industrialized, capitalist societies (not as much in Mexico, for example, where Bellatín was born, but even more so in countries such as England, Germany, France and the United States) have an inherent intolerance for death because it gets in the way of the great industrial/capitalist plan. One must avoid its ugliness at all costs. It appears that Bellatín has reached over to the east as an orientalist writer to find a place where he can explore the beauty of his own death, and to keep the process of his death in what Barthes calls the "perpetual present" (5) without feeling as though this need is necessarily a negative thing. The fact that he often keeps the countries and cities of his novels unnamed has created an open space to explore one's death without having to be trapped by the cultural expectations surrounding it. In this sense, the author allows the reader to have some open space to explore death, illness and beauty without cultural judgment. He uses what Donoso Macaya calls "mutilación lingüística" (105) by using vocabularies from other languages perhaps as a way to come to grips with his haunting ideas of bodily mutilation. Tsurumi also notes that Bellatín reaches "a level of decontextualization that allows him to freely confront the dilemmas of artistic creation" (131) without necessarily creating an autobiography. Part of his bold artistic confrontation with linguistic mutilation and auto-fiction is that he openly admits to not conducting cultural research before writing his culturally hybrid novels. But in order to give freedom to the reader, the author paradoxically creates numerous characters that are bound to enclosed spaces with nothing more than their own bodies and repetitive memories of death and ghosts to tell their stories. The novelist has created worlds where social status is recognized but not given as much weight as the organic life of a garden or the process of writing or suffering through the body's process of decay.

It is interesting how photography comes into play with artistic intentions of Mario Bellatín. It is said that photography is supposed to show truth and maintain immortality, and, at the same time, the novels presented in this chapter have been created to do the exact opposite. Both *Shiki Nagaoka: Una nariz de ficción* and *La clase muerta* rely heavily on photographs to "prove" that their stories are true. Bellatín's novels strive to undo photography and its quest for truth and immortality by focusing on fiction and mortality as being the realities of each of the protagonists in these novels. In *La clase muerta*, (another novel that presents the interesting mix of Japanese and German cultures), the narrator describes undeveloped film as images that never actually existed. Incidentally, the camera is another autobiographical signature of Bellatín, who in his article "Underwood Portátil. Modelo 1915" wrote about a camera given to him as a child. Interestingly, this camera and its images also appeared in the hallucinations of the sick man in *Disecado*, although in *Disecado* the reader is never given the visual content that can be found in *La clase muerta* and *Shiki Nagaoka*.[42]

Another common theme found in several novels is the theme of ritual. In *La clase muerta* the narrator describes el *ritual de las luciérnagas* where toothless women buried themselves alive after finding a stone in their rice. While it is difficult to know if this tradition truly exists, the addition of such an obscure detail is one more way that Bellatín insists that his readers do some of their own work when participating in his art form. In Roland Barthes's *S/Z* (1974), the theorist states that "the goal of a literary work is to make the reader no longer a consumer, but a producer of text" (4). There is no way of knowing how much of Barthes can be found in the artistic psyche of Bellatín, but it is certain that he does not want his readers to simply "consume" his work, but rather participate in it, and perhaps take a look at their own truths and rituals as well as their own deaths and decide for themselves what is fictional and what is not. The rituals of the monks exchanging shoes or jumping into deep water to feel the urgency of rising to the surface is also an interesting example of fictional spirituality that Bellatín weaves into his narrative in *La clase muerta*. Another ritual that appears to be fictional is the "peregrinación anual al Valle de la Luna" in *El jardín de la señora Murakami*, where Izu's mother leaves home for several days each year to honor the dead child she lost in the war. The descriptions of these rituals are all very similar to the pages of labeled photos found in *Shiki Nagaoka* and *La clase muerta*. They lead the reader to wonder, to doubt, even to research if these things are true, yet when it is discovered that it is all in fictional jest, it adds richness to the work instead of providing

---

42 For further reading on the concept of the photographic novel, please see the article "Entre palabras e imágenes: las fotografías como dispositivo metaficcional en 'Tinísima' de Elena Poniatowska" by Magdalena Perkowska.

a sense of deception for the invested reader.

Other than the mention of Izu's dead baby brother, it is not common to find children as regular parts of Mario Bellatín's works. The figure of the parent, the spouse, or even the imaginary friend is more common. Any children in these novels are adult children who have parents that have been reduced to childhood, usually through age or illness. In *La clase muerta*, Joao cares for his mother until her death, just as Izu does for her father and her husband. Perhaps this lack of babies and children in these novels is connected to the author's insistence on the lack of origin, the insistence on not telling the reader exactly from where the protagonists are coming (except for a few exceptions, such as Joao and his mother in Brazil). The author is incredibly open about the origins of many of his ideas, and he does refer to his own childhood indirectly several times, but perhaps a world where phantom limbs, garden ghosts, and headless monks dwell is not the same place where children wander in their imaginations. Perhaps Bellatín is making the point that we never actually stop being children. The fears, dreams, and insecurities that the protagonists face in his works could be considered childish; the fact that sexual love is not a theme at the forefront of these novels could also be a sign that the labyrinths within which we are working are actually creations of childhood imagination. The fact that death is not final is also something that many children perceive as reality; understanding the finality of death is one of the more painful parts of becoming an adult, and it appears that the majority of the protagonists in these four novels do not have a sense that death is final. If they do, it does not appear to cause them considerable pain. Moreover, the playfulness, the absurdity, and the quality of the photos in the book all lend themselves to the possibility of being work done by a person with a child's flexible sense of reality and magic. But the worlds constructed in these novels are also frightening places for children, where men like Señor Murakami sell girls' underwear to perverts on the black market, and then eat rolls to increase their sexual appetite before walking by the zoo and the kindergarten, or where the fish in the tank in *Disecado* first eat the male fish and then eat all of the baby fish and die. Worse, when the Bellatín's reality comes to light that "lo único cierto en la vida era un hueco… un espacio vacio" (*La clase muerta* 38) the author makes a very shocking yet poignant point that children do actually live in the same disgusting and terrible world of adults, but perhaps the knowledge of life's one truth (emptiness) has not yet broken them the way it has many adults. It appears that the author is fixated not on the total life cycle (birth, life, death) but more one a specific aspect of the life cycle, which includes the isolation and pain of death and dying, more so than the focus on creation, origin, and childhood.

Many other authors from Latin America use Orientalism as part of their constructions of fiction, it might be worth exploring some of the older examples of Orientalist writing as having been possibly influential in the formation of Bellatín as an Orientalist writer. Traces from the works of authors such as Rubén Darío and Jorge Luis Borges, for example, seem particularly poignant when studying more recent novels such as the ones discussed in this chapter. While it is uncertain to what degree Bellatín has studied these authors, there are certainly similarities within their work that would make one believe that these authors are influential in his narrative choices. Darío uses the image of the garden as a basis to explore greed and death in his short story "El rey burgués". The bourgeois king has a garden and a capricious collection of Asian artifacts that entertain him but that do not necessarily convey meaning or emotional value for him. A poet comes to him and is left to die in his garden playing a music box. While Darío labels this "un cuento alegre", the irony is that the story is terribly sad and shows judgment on those who find superficial value in art and poetry. Bellatín's work lacks this same kind of emotional judgment (in fact, even in the face of death, Bellatín is rather emotionless), yet it is hard to escape the descriptive similarities that one finds when reading about Señora Murakami's garden, for example. In "El rey burgués", both the king and the poet could be representative of both Señor and/or Señora Murakami; like Señor Murakami, the king keeps a collection that includes a human enclosed in a garden. The poet (not the king) dies in the end but this does not insist in any way that the king himself is immortal. The king (like Señora Muraka-mi) is left with a garden and has witnessed a death without expressing any extreme outer emotion, but again, in no way does Bellatín give any indication that this lack of emotion means that Señora Murakami is exempt from a similar fate to her husband's. The only thing that seems like it could endure beyond precious objects, human life, and even poetry could be the garden, where the beginnings and ends of nature's process are witnessed without words or emotions, enclosed and kept hidden from outside influence.

Bellatín's mockery of himself in his work is very similar to Jorge Luis Borges. The two authors have very similar manners of using stories set in the Orient to flesh out the larger questions at stake regarding reality, life, death and dreams. This style of writing can be described as being like a labyrinth; the reader twists and turns between past and present, dreams and wakeful hours, the dead and the living, only to arrive at a destiny that seems as though it was evident from the beginning. The center of Bellatín's work (as well as in Borges' work) "awakens a feeling of resignation and a willingness to accept death, possibly because the alternative, once perceived, is too horrible to accept" (Dauster 144). All of the characters in the Bellatín novels discussed in this chapter have either already died, or have had endless brushes with death, or have doubtful connections with reality itself. The protagonists are often overwhelmingly emotionless, hopeless, and do not seem capable of feeling love. Frank Dauster says of Borges' characters something very similar:

> It is noteworthy that those who reach the center of the labyrinth, i.e., who perceive the meaning of their own existence, almost invariably die. Furthermore, they die resigned, recognizing that their existence no longer has significance. There is more than a hint that this recognition is caused, at least in part, by the realization of the horror of the universe (147).

Several of Borges' works include gardens and labyrinths, and inevitably characters who die or see ghosts in their midst. Yet both Borges and Bellatín are playful in their reflections on the horrors of the universe, both by creating strange, yet real, characters (Shiki Nagaoka with his large nose, for example), and particularly in Bellatín's case, with the use of photography. The photographs that make up significant parts of his books are strange, silly and quite clearly fictional, yet they add to the uncanny feeling that one could be looking at their own family album and realizing that they themselves are dead or not real. Both authors are also playful with language, including several languages in their Spanish texts that interact with one another. Yet this playfulness is up against constant images of enclosure, erasure, destruction of books, objects and people, where human beings seek to flee death and only end up becoming death itself or inflicting it carelessly on themselves or another. Unlike Bellatín, Borges preoccupies himself with questions of origin (in "Las ruinas circulars," for example, when a man creates a kind of Adam or in "La muralla y los libros" when an emperor tries to erase all origin before his own by building a wall and burning books). Yet all of these characters who try to build greatness inevitably die, and it appears that both Borges and Bellatín are acutely aware that their deaths will be the result of the numerous labyrinths, dreams, and nameless worlds that they create with their writing.

Bellatín and Borges share many similarities particularly in Borges' short story "El jardín de senderos que se bifurcan" (1941). In this story, the theme of the labyrinth being connected to the creative process of writing and books is evident. Also, like several of Bellatín's works, it combines several characters from different cultures in the story, including England, Germany, Ireland and China. Like *Disecado*, "El jardín de senderos que se bifurcan" begins with a man lying on a bed contemplating his own death. The protagonist knows that he will die and he also knows that he possesses an important Secret. Again, we are able to see how both Bellatín and Borges can take a drab and ordinary setting and turn it into something mysterious and filled with curiosity and even magic. Also like Bellatín, in the story by Borges there is only a brief mention of children. Their faces are in shadow, and then they disappear. The protagonist talks of his childhood gardens, his dead father, and the fact that he is a cowardly man with a weak voice, and therefore he had to use his weakness in order to conjure up strength (perhaps the same way Borges and Bellatín use writing to overcome their own perceived weaknesses?). The strange man that Borges' protagonist visits, Stephen Albert, explains the key to the novel that never ends, like a garden with many forking paths. This is how both Borges and Bellatín approach their writing; they do not want a specific solution or answer at the end of their works. They do not want to simply serve a piece of literature to be consumed by their readers. Both writers, I believe, show in their works that the best kind of narrative is the one that does not have only one possible ending, and that a good reader is one who explores the infinite possibilities of the many possible meanings behind the ending. Similar to the "incomprehensible" book that Shiki Nagaoka left behind after his death, Ts'ui Pen in Borges' story does the same thing. In both works, the "auto-fictional" families are outraged, people are confused, critics call their works the ramblings of madmen. But I believe that both Borges and Bellatín would agree that only those who know how to read into a text would be able to decipher such works and truly come out of their literary labyrinths alive.

Riger Tsurumi writes well when she describes the magic of Bellatín (and I would say that these words could also be applied to Borges): "Mario Bellatín wraps himself in the traditions of distant foreign cultures like a magician's cloak of invisibility that enables him to reflect on important questions about literature and uncover truths about the act of writing and the role of the writer in his texts" (131). The novels discussed in this chapter are thought-provoking on the level of character and plot development; yet it is also important to remember the larger questions brought to light by the author's Orientalist style; the role of the writer and the reader should both be active when participating in the development of a novel, and in the case of Mario Bellatín, this goal is achieved with both grit and grace as he pushes his readers to make connections between east and west, and between what is perceived as fiction and what is considered reality.

BIBLIOGRAPHY

Ariés, Philipe. *Western Attitudes toward Death: From the Middle Ages to the Present*. Trans. Patricia M. Ranum. Baltimore: Johns Hopkins University Press, 1974. Print.

Barthes, Roland. *S/Z*. Trans. Richard Miller. Malden: Blackwell Publishing, 1974. Print.

Bellatín, Mario. *La clase muerta: dos textos*. Mexico: Alfaguara, 2011. Print.

—. *Disecado*. Mexico: Sexto Piso Editorial, 2011. Print.

—. *El jardín de la Señora Murakami*. México: Tusquets Editores, 2000. Print.

—. *Shiki Nagaoka: Una nariz de ficción*. Buenos Aires: Editorial Sudamericana, 2001. Print.

—. "Underwood Portátil. Modelo 1915." *La novela según los novelistas*. Ed. Cristina Rivera Garza. México, D.F.: Fondo de Cultura Económica, 2007. Web. 159-178.

Borges, Jorge Luis. "El jardín de senderos que se bifurcan." Literatura.us. Web. 5 July, 2012.

—. "Los dos reyes y los dos laberintos." *Ciudad Seva*. La Biblioteca Digital Ciudad Seva, 10 Nov. 2010. Web. 19 Mar. 2012.

Darío, Rubén. "El rey burgués. Cuento alegre." *Cuidad Seva*. La Biblioteca Digital Ciudad Seva, 10 Nov. 2010. Web. 13 Mar. 2012.

Dauster, Frank. "Notes on Borges' Labyrinths." *Hispanic Review* 30.2 (1962): 142-148. Print.

Donoso Macaya, Ángeles. "'Yo soy Mario Bellatín y soy de ficción' o el paradójico borde de lo autobiográfico en *El gran vidrio (2007)*." *Chasqui: Revista de Literatura Latinoamericana* 40.1 (2011): 96-110. Print.

Friis, Ronald J. "'The Fury and the Mire of Human Veins': Frida Kahlo and Rosario Castellanos." *Hispania* 87.1 (2004): 53-61. Print.

Giorgi, Gabriel and Karen Pinkus. "Zones of Exception: Biopolitical Territories in the Neoliberal Era." *Bios, Immunity, Life: The Thought of Robert Esposito*. Spec. issue of *Diacritics* 36.2 (2006): 99-108. Print.

Gorer, Geoffrey. "The Pornography of Death." *Encounter*, Oct. 1955: 49-52. Web.

Holloway, James E. Jr. "'La escritura del dios' de Borges: cómo escapa el encarcelado de su prisión ilusoria." *Revista Canadiense de Estudios Hispánicos* 28.2 (2004): 333-354. Print.

Jurado, Alicia. Estudio preliminar. *Páginas de Jorge Luis Borges: seleccionadas por el autor.* By Jorge Luis Borges. Ed. Alicia Jurado. Buenos Aires: Editorial Celtia, 1983. Print.

Kushigian, Julia A. *Orientalism in the Hispanic Literary Tradition. In Dialogue with Borges, Paz, and Sarduy.* Albuquerque: University of New Mexico Press, 1991. Print.

Menocal, María Rosa. "Blindness: Alephs and Lovers." *Jorge Luis Borges.* Ed. Harold Bloom. Philadelphia: Chelsea House Publishers, 2004. 91-132. Print.

Palaversich, Diana. "Apuntes para una lectura de Mario Bellatín." *Chasqui: Revista de Literatura Latinoamericana.* 32.1 (2003): 25-38. Print.

Perkowska, Magdalena. "Entre palabras e imágenes: las fotografías como dispositivo metaficcional en 'Tinísima' de Elena Poniatoska". *Ciberletras* 19 (July 2008): n. pag. Web. 4 February 2013.

Tsurumi, Rebecca Riger. *The Closed Hand: Images of the Japanese in Modern Peruvian Literature.* West Lafayette, Indiana: Purdue University Press, 2012. Print.

ELLA, YO Y EL *YOTRO*: ORIENTALISMS AND IDENTITIES IN CRISTINA RIVERA GARZA'S *VERDE SHANGHAI*

JENNIFER PRINCE

> *La historia solo tiene sentido dentro de otra historia.*
> Cristina Rivera Garza, *Verde Shanghai*

> *Con alivio, con humillación, con terror, comprendió que él*
> *también era una apariencia, que otro estaba soñándolo.*
> Jorge Luis Borges, "Las ruinas circulares"

In 1991, Mexican author Cristina Rivera Garza published a book of short stories: *La guerra no importa*. The stories of the book are thematically similar, but they are further linked by a recurring corpus of characters and a unifying, underlying plot. The author conceived the stories as part of a greater narrative and imagined writing a novel later that utilizes *La guerra no importa* as its base (Hind 192). *Verde Shanghai*, published twenty years after its precursor, is the realization of that novel with the short stories of *La guerra no importa* largely preserved in their original forms. Additional narrative written by Rivera Garza serves to interweave the stories even more.

In 1969, Rafael Bernal published *El complot mongol*, a detective novel that has since become a classic in contemporary Mexican literature. The novel, which concerns an investigation into a plot to assassinate the President of the United States, is partially situated in the *barrio chino* of Mexico City, where the plot is said to have originated. Bernal's publication has ushered in an era of other contemporary Latin American novels that have demonstrated an interest in the meeting of Hispanic cultures with Asian ones, specifically Chinese. This trend has produced several well-received publications in the past ten years. Some of these novels, like *Los impostores* (2002) by the Colombian author Santiago Gamboa or *El ombligo del dragón* (2007) by Ximena Sánchez Echenique from Mexico, feature the experiences of Latin American characters abroad in China. Yet other novels place the meeting of Hispanic and Asian cultures in Latin America. Featuring another cosmopolitan Latin American capital, *Un chino en bicicleta*, a comedic novel published in 2007 by Ariel Magnus, follows the story of a young Argentinian kidnapped by a Chinese man and who later becomes immersed in the world of the barrio chino of Buenos Aires. Cristina Rivera Garza's novel, *Verde Shanghai* (2011), also explores the relationship of Latin Americans and Chinese and, like *El complot mongol*, is set in the barrio chino of Mexico City.

In *Verde Shanghai*, the novel's protagonist, Marina Espinosa, is a woman living an uninteresting yet comfortable life married to a wealthy doctor, Horacio Oligochea. After a car accident that leaves her with a broken arm, Marina is haunted by the image of another woman whose name Marina knows—she's called Xian—but whose identity remains a mystery. Marina believes that knowing Xian will help her understand more about her own identity, so she begins to search the neighborhood where she knows Xian lives: the barrio chino of the capital. In doing this, Marina leaves behind her previous life, much to the consternation of her husband, and submerges herself completely in a new, marginal, and oriental world. The search for Xian reflects Marina's search for herself and the married woman begins to discover her own identity while discovering her voice, previously silenced for many years in a relationship with Horacio that is typified by Marina keeping quiet and not revealing any personal information to her husband. Marina recuperates memories of the past and her voice in an exchange of writings with a Chinese interlocutor, Chiang Wei, who also uses his written dialogue with Marina to explore his own past.

In interviews, Rivera Garza repeatedly has mentioned her attraction and desire to create literature that poses questions more than it provides answers so that the readers have a space to create their own meaning and their own answers

(Hind 188; Samuelson, "Writing" 141). This demand on the reader has also been recognized by critics like Rafael Lemus in his review of the novel as he indicates that some readers may not be totally convinced by the complexities and twists and turns in the story. Yet in *Verde Shanghai*, Rivera Garza achieves the goal she set out to accomplish, composing a novel that tantalizes the limits of language and structure in order to create a world where nothing can be known for certain. Names are changed, confused, or non-existent and identities are ambiguous, transient, temporary. Lemus describes this chaos as "[a]lgo que sobra o falta, cierta inestabilidad, cabos no atados, recursos no pulidos, ambiciones desmesuradas, huecos, fracturas, un no sé qué que extraña." While the critic admits all this, he reveals that it all contributes to the interest that Rivera Garza creates as an author. *Verde Shanghai*, in my opinion, is not just a novel that makes a reader interested, but rather puts a spell on its readers: taunting them with the questions and just a hint of an answer, making them believe that there was something they missed and if they just read again they might find a solution. Beyond the charm for a casual reader, the questions and the complexities of the book—according to Lemus, with whom I am in agreement—create a richness that makes the work of Rivera Garza ripe for critical analysis.

Out of all the questions that *Verde Shanghai* raises, the most important of all—Exactly what is the real relationship between Marina and Xian?—probably has as many possible answers as there are readers of the novel. Although often many passages of the book remain unclear with limited or confusing details, three relationships in *Verde Shanghai* especially stand out, even if it cannot be said that they leave little room for questions and doubt. These three relationships—between Horacio and Marina, Marina and Chiang, and finally, between Marina and Xian—are the focus of this study. Each of these relationships highlights shades of orientalisms during Marina's search for her identity.

Horacio/Marina: Orientalization and domination

In his influential book, *Orientalism*, Edward Said proposes a dichotomy of East and West that is a relationship of power, with the Occident dominating the Orient, but also is a way for the Occident to define itself (1-2). A person's or a group's identity is generally forged by affirming the differences between "us" and the "Other" with this difference helping to construct a hierarchy (Mouffe 6). In Said's orientalist theory, the established hierarchy proposes that the West is simply superior to the East, and this feeling of superiority—as well as the differences that establish it—is cemented as hegemony (5). Because the Occident sees itself as a place of logical and rational beings aided by advanced knowledge in the scientific and philosophic realms, the Orient must be completely the opposite. The people of the Orient are weak of mind, without the ability to reason (38-40). Furthermore, according to the West, the people of Asia shouldn't even be making their own decisions. They are a "subject race, dominated by a race that knows them and what is good for them better than they could possibly know themselves" (35). So the West, due to its innate superiority, not only has the *right* to control the East, but because of their benevolence and sense of duty to the less fortunate they also have the *responsibility* to do it.

The relationship between Horacio and his wife, Marina, is an orientalist relationship typical of what Said describes. A subject, believing to have knowledge and power on his side, dominates an object. As was already mentioned, the marriage of Horacio and Marina is rather bland and, while Marina generally is a quiet and compliant participant in matrimony, the orientalist imbalance of the relationship doesn't manifest itself until Marina begins her quest to find Xian. The search for the other woman is a process of orientalization for Marina; she begins to spend her days in the barrio chino of the city, frequenting a Chinese café called "Verde Shanghai" and speaking with the Chinese people that live and work in the neighborhood.

The change in his wife does not go unnoticed by Horacio, who begins to question Marina's health and judgment.

As a doctor, and therefore well trained in modern science and medicine, Horacio epitomizes the man of the Occident. After her accident, Marina's behavior changes to the opposite of what Horacio considers normal or Occidental. In becoming the opposite, Marina is becoming Oriental. Horacio notices the change and begins to study her with a medical and scientific gaze, questioning her mental health. The change in his perception of her is so obvious that it is even reflected in a change of name for Marina. For the first time, Horacio calls her "Mar" (88), an image of the sea that is evoked again soon after in associating Marina with the sounds of a northern ocean. So when Marina begins to orientalize herself, Horacio begins to think of her as someone unknown and different, as an Other.

This Other becomes increasingly objectified to Horacio. After she refuses to see a psychiatric specialist at Horacio's request, Marina becomes sick with pneumonia and returns home feverish and delirious. The doctor greets her with her new name: "—Mar [...] Estás ardiendo en fiebre –diagnosticó de inmediato" (99). Horacio treats Marina as if she were "alguien que acababa de dejar el hospital después de una cirugía mayor" (99). This treatment of the doctor is only the first step to her objectification, however, and there is an increase in Horacio's fixation on Marina's body. While Marina suffers in a fevered delirium, Horacio has the desire to take photographs of her, fascinated by the way the illness leaves the body without consciousness, "en esa dominación absoluta del cuerpo" (100). The passage that follows exemplifies the complete conversion of Marina the wife into a body, an unknown woman, an object for photos and for study:

> Horacio [...] colocó la cámara fotográfica sobre el tripié y encendió el disparador automático. Luego se dispuso a iniciar su tarea. La descobijó y, hablándole en voz baja, la desnudó por completo. Manipulaba su cuerpo con precaución, como si temiera despertarla de su trance por equivocación.

> Poco a poco, sin dejar de arrullarla con su lenguaje,
> la colocó sobre el hombro izquierdo para poder in-
> yectarla en la esquina exterior derecha del glúteo.
> Una gota de sangre sobre la piel de la mujer y, en su
> entorno, el ruido incesante, perfecto, de la cámara
> fotográfica. (101)

The medical study of his wife does not end there, however. When the delirious Marina begins to murmur a string of words, a fascinated Horacio begins to transcribe "el lenguaje de su enfermedad," acting as "el científico que requiere de evidencias para comprobar una hipótesis" (104).

Although Horacio sees Marina's orientalization only as a sickness, it seems like the process is one of liberation for Marina, a chance to find her own voice and her own identity. While she was living with Horacio, she was nearly silent. In fact, her husband believed that "[l]a verdad de Marina era el silencio" (100). This all changed with her feverish mumblings the night she got pneumonia. When Marina is finally well, she disappears into the barrio chino, beginning a new phase of her life. She spends her days writing her story and exchanging its pages with those of her newfound interlocutor, Chiang. This dialogue will be the subject of more investigation later.

Marina's free will and self-governance is curtailed when Horacio discovers her whereabouts. The rational, scientific, Occidental doctor sees his wife as unable to make her own decisions about how to live her life. Horacio displays his right and his responsibility to govern his wife when one night he sends a pair of men to nearly kidnap his wife from the hotel and bring her back to his home. He insists that she doesn't feel well and that bringing her home "[e]s mi responsabilidad" (293). Furthermore, he adds: "[e]ntendería si no estuvieras de acuerdo. Es más, sé que no estás de acuerdo. Pero era mi deber" (294).

Even though the relationship between Marina and Horacio appears to end with the domination of male over female, subject over Other, and she seems to accept it, readers shouldn't just assume that Said's theory of orientalism is what definitively and negatively colors Marina's oriental experience. On the contrary, the period of time when Marina is "orientalized" is presented as a time of great liberation and of self-discovery. She is searching for an identity and finally begins to feel free to express herself. Furthermore, the more complex oriental relationships featured during the time of orientalization are a major focus of the book. These other two relationships have little to do with orientalisms as Said describes them and reflect the much more complicated relationship that exists between the Hispanic culture and the Orient. As Julia Kushigian explains in her book, *Orientalism in the Hispanic Literary Tradition*, Hispanic Orientalism is much more diverse, more multi-faceted than the Orientalism as described by Said, because of "a much more profound historical and intellectual contact with the Orient" (1-2). Or, as described by Araceli Tinajero in *Orientalismo en el modernismo hispanoamericano*, the dialogue between Hispanic America and the East is a dialogue between two groups both considered the "periphery" by the Eurocentric West (20). Hispanic Orientalism is an exchange between two Others.

Marina/Chiang: Interlocutors Investigating Identities

Marina comes to know Chiang Wei, the grandson of a Chinese immigrant and Marina's future interlocutor, in an agreement with doña Aída, the owner of the café "Verde Shanghai." Although Marina enters into the agreement hoping to discover more about herself by meeting Xian—doña Aída promises to introduce the two if Marina meets Chiang first—the Chinese man becomes important to helping Marina establish her identity. Marina and Chiang establish a dialogue, not through speaking necessarily, but through writing the stories of their own pasts.

In their article "Narrating the Self," anthropologist Elinor Ochs and psychologist Lisa Capps examine the importance of narratives to establish identities, make sense of the world, and connect the past, present, and an imagined and hypothetical universe (22). According to the two authors, narratives not only help narrators and listener/readers "navigate relationships with others" (21), but they also provide the "opportunity for fragmented self-understanding" (22). So many narrators begin their narratives "in response to current worries, complaints, and conflicts" (25), which is certainly the case for Marina, who can't remember or doesn't want to remember her past. This lack of memory of the past, a lack of continuity between the past and the present, makes Marina's own identity inaccessible to her, as the preexistence of an identity with its experiences, emotions, and behavior allow for the construction of a present identity (29, 22-23).

In Kushigian's book, she proposes that Hispanic Orientalism "is committed to opening a dialogue and exchange with the East for the purpose of learning about the self from the Other, revealing truth through dialogue and ending cultural domination" (3). This dialogue with Chiang is necessary for Marina as it is the opportunity for her to discover her narrative and therefore her identity. When Marina begins to orientalize herself, she also begins to write. A desire to tell her story consumes her, although previously, with Horacio, she had requested that he never ask her about her past. The day that Chiang first reveals something from his own past, however, Marina decides it is time for her to share as well. What Chiang recounts to Marina is the recollection of the day he first saw Marina as a baby, the day when their future marriage was contracted. Marina is stunned and incredulous at this revelation, despite already having heard of the supposed arrangement from the mouth of doña Aída in their first meeting. But the story is an impetus for Marina to begin a dialogue with Chiang, as if the possibility of being declared Chiang's bride in a time long before makes Marina want to remember and examine her *own* real history. Yet with the first written story that she offers to Chiang, Marina also reveals her confusion as to whether it is about her own past or the past of another.

Chiang recognizes the importance of their narratives and pasts in establishing their existences. With Marina he shares the story of his grandfather's arrival in the country intercalated with archival material and research about the difficult history of the Chinese people in Mexico and the harsh treatment they received. Chiang does all this for the reason of establishing identity, telling Marina: "Quiero que creas tu propia historia, Marina. Tu historia conmigo. Y quiero que la creas porque de otra manera ni tú ni yo existimos" (177).

While Marina's first offering of her past, the first pages of her story, were presented tentatively and without any certainty that they actually represented her past, Chiang's stories seem to open a door in Marina's mind, awakening *something* that takes days to manifest itself but finally liberates Marina's past:

> Supuso que algo había pasado en los años que trataba de recordar, en efecto. […] Algo.
> Por días enteros pensó en eso, en Algo.
> Salía del cuarto del hotel con Algo en la mente. Y Algo la obligaba a caminar sin rumbo por horas enteras. […] Con el tiempo, Algo se volvió su compañía más asidua. Así, con Algo a su lado, volvió a abrir el libro que le anclaba la memoria y, con Algo vigilándola sobre los hombros, se dispuso a seguir con la única tarea en la que Algo se expandía. (183)

What follows are pages and pages of Marina's memories from her youth that she has typed, incited by the Something that is haunting her.

Chiang Wei had commented previously that beginnings are always the hardest part (171). In the dialogue between him and Marina, Chiang does that hard work so that the doors are opened for Marina's story to be revealed more easily. Thus, their dialogue follows the theory of Kushigian. Marina brings her Other, Chiang, closer to herself and then is able to think about her own identity. Her relationship with Chiang and the initial discomfort and confusion in their dialogue allows Marina to leave "the familiar and secure to be able to transcend them and ultimately assess" herself (14). Just like doña Aída promised, through her relationship with Chiang, Marina is also able to know Xian.

Marina/Xian: One and the Other are One and the Same?

Physically, there is never a complete description of Xian in *Verde Shanghai*, although Marina's appearance as well is never detailed. Xian's identification as an oriental Other comes from her obviously Chinese name, her frequent location—the barrio chino—and the fact that Marina finds similarities between Xian and Chiang. To Marina, Xian is obviously mysterious and alluring, creating a desire in the former to find her and discover her secret, a secret that Marina believes will reveal something about her own identity as well. While the relationship between the two women could have many possible explanations, one of the most intriguing and one that answers many questions that the book raises is that Xian and Marina are the same person. Indeed, Rafael Lemus believes this to be true in his review of the novel, but the connection isn't explicitly made and—in the complexity typical of Rivera Garza—leaves room for doubt

There are many clues left by the author, consciously or not, that support the idea of the double or split identity. Ambiguous sentences and the repeated confusion of names, especially Marina's and Xian's, obfuscate the line between where one woman ends and the other begins. Often characters see Marina and call her Xian. Furthermore, immediately following her accident, Marina sees Xian but she also begins to notice, to think about, *something* new. "Dentro de su cabeza, algo, el tiempo. Algo detenido como el tiempo a las 6:10 de la tarde. Algo que se llamaba Xian" (35). Is this the same Something that later sits across from Marina as she writes, provoking her, inciting her memory, and making her write more? Is this Something called Xian a part of Marina that emerges to help Marina question and investigate her own existence?

While these questions can't be immediately answered, the issues raised by doña Aída's recognition of Marina as a member of the Chou family, as well as the assertion of the sage woman and Chiang Wei that Marina was to be married to Chiang, could both be explained if Marina is an oriental

Other. Even Chiang—a man who, unlike Horacio, really begins to know Marina—questions her identity as Marina. "No eres tú, Marina. [...] Estoy seguro que no eres tú" (159-160). Marina responds, saying: "*Je es un autre*," and the two interlocutors decide that the word *Yotro* best describes this new concept (160-161).

Yotro. The combination of I and Other is a promising explanation for the relationship between Marina and Xian. But even this answer, keeping with the now-familiar style of Rivera Garza, also raises more questions. Is the *Yo* Marina and the *Otro* Xian? Or is it the other way around?

The work of Ochs and Capps supports the idea that the original *Yo* is Xian. The two authors posit that conditions such as post-traumatic stress disorder, depression, and anxiety can silence a narrative that connects the present to the past (33), erasing past narratives from memory. It is possible that a young Xian—after witnessing the traffic accident that killed an intimate friend, Julia—silenced her past narratives, therefore eliminating the identity of Xian and assuming a new identity, that of Marina. The past becomes alien to Marina; she can't or won't speak of it, as evidenced by her request of Horacio that he never asks her about the time before they met. When Marina suffers a serious accident on the street similar to the one that killed her friend, she begins to experience fragments of memories of Xian and her past, reflected in the fragments of text used in the novel. When these fragments begin to surface, they are confusing to Marina and prompt her search for an interlocutor to help her sort out her narrative. Ochs and Capps explain that "[n]arrative activity is crucial to recognizing and integrating repressed and alienated selves" (30). Furthermore, "Each telling of a narrative situated in time and space engages only facets of a narrator's or listener/reader's selfhood in that it evokes only certain memories, concerns, and expectations. [...] In this sense, narratives are apprehended by *partial* selves, and narratives so apprehended access only fragments of experience" (22). So as Marina reconstructs the narratives of her past, Xian begins to exist again, but the identities are still fragmented, especially at first, because narratives have the possibility to generate multiple fragmented selves.

The second possible *Yotro* combination is that Marina is the *Yo* and Xian is the *Otro*. Judith Butler, in her book *Gender Trouble*, questions the idea that identity is singular and unified, always persisting through time without changing (22). She wonders:

> To what extent is 'identity' a normative ideal rather than a descriptive feature of experience? And how do the regulatory practices that govern gender also govern culturally intelligible notions of identity? In other words, the 'coherence' and 'continuity' of 'the person' are not logical or analytic features of personhood, but, rather, socially instituted and maintained norms of intelligibility. (23)

Ochs and Capps echo Butler's idea, saying that society expects narratives, which are what form identity, to reinforce social order (33). As an upper middle class woman and the wife of a doctor, Marina is expected to behave as such. That is her identity, her narrative that must not vary. Butler even states that identifying people as women is "a refusal to grant freedom and autonomy to women as it is purportedly enjoyed by men" (27). This lack of freedom is obvious in the case of Marina, who exists mostly in silence while completing her duties as a wife and a woman of a certain socioeconomic standing. It is natural, then, that she would look for a chance to break free of that oppression.

For Marina, Xian is a being not confined by the same restraints that shackle an upper middle class woman. As an Other, Xian is already marginalized by virtue of being Oriental and living in the barrio chino. But living a marginalized life among other marginalized people provides Xian with the freedom to live life as she sees fit. The difference between the two women is attractive to Marina and so she seeks out Xian as a way of finding her own freedom. As Kushigian explains:

> An evocation of the Other will also bring the distanced image closer as it precipitates a way to examine one's existence, one's being-in-the-world.

The ensuing antithetical movement of acceptance and rejection of the Other reinforces the difficult process [...] of leaving the familiar and secure to be able to transcend them and ultimately assess oneself. *The Other is theoretically "created" to explain the self.* (14, emphasis added)

Although Kushigian is not speaking literally of the creation of another being, this quotation posits an intriguing option: Marina creates Xian through creating Xian's narrative as a way to establish a separate, more liberated identity. As Marina searches for her alter ego, Xian, she enters the neighborhood where Xian would be and weaves the stories of Xian's past into her own. While becoming closer to her other identity, she marginalizes herself as she orientalizes herself, but both provide her the opportunity to lead a life not governed by social constraints or her husband.

Laberintos y Ruinas Circulares: Oblivion and Reality

Both previous explanations of the possible link between Xian and Marina, while rooted in critical theory and commonly held beliefs about reality, are insufficient. The explanations seem incomplete and always propose further questions rather than neatly providing one solution to all problems. A recurring theme in *Verde Shanghai* is the questioning of existence, wondering whether certain people are the inventions of others. Both Marina and Xian declare and confirm their own existence; they are skeptical about the existence of the other, however. The two women separately ponder reasons for the other's presence in their lives—insanity, a dream, an invention, a memory—but cannot give a reasonable explanation for why the other is as undoubtedly real as they are themselves. Xian's most complete explanation is that "[r]ecordar [...] es un asunto complicado. Los recuerdos cobran vida por sí mismos y, sin parpadear, sin preocuparse por aquellos que los generaron, adquieren piernas, manos, caras, voces" (219).

The 20th Century Argentinian author Jorge Luis Borges wrote many stories with themes concerning the Orient. Two of these stories—"Las ruinas circulares" (1940) and "El jardín de los senderos que se bifurcan" (1941)—are included in the aptly named anthology *Ficciones* (1944) and can contribute much to the discussion of *Verde Shanghai*. In a conversation with Chiang, Marina refers to the human body as a fiction. But how is it possible to conceive of one's own body, physical, material, as fiction?

In her chapter on Borges, Kushigian notes that the Orient in his works is often presented as a metaphor for "for infinite time, fantasy, and utopia" (19). Kushigian continues, explaining that Borges's utopias are actually heterotopias, able to "order and destroy order simultaneously" (22).[43] Furthermore, the dialogue created in the conversation between the utopic Orient and the realist Occident serves a purpose of "go[ing] beyond limits of time and space to attract the reader into yet one more labyrinth, or to see the reader's image of the Orient reflected again in the infinitely shifting mirrors, or to examine metaphysically another ordered image of wholeness" (19).

Borges himself writes that reality in literature tends to follow one of three different types, the second of which "consiste en imaginar una realidad más compleja que la declarada al lector y referir sus derivaciones y efectos" ("La postulación" 71). Sylvia Molloy adds that this postulation "relies on literary suggestion, on the blurring of limits. It tempts the reader with the illusion of what has not been said, with the never explicit promise of new openings, of secondary stories" (65). This type of clash between the Orient and the Occident, utopia and heterotopia, real and irreal, as well as an invitation into a

---

43 To make this point, Kushigian uses the chapter "Borges and the Latin-American Text" from Julio Ortega's *Poetics of Change* (1984) which examines utopia in Borges's works while discarding Michel Foucault's analysis of utopias. According to Ortega: "Contrary to what he [Foucault] states, utopias are not comforting […]. They do not imply an improbable place and time but a virtual language, one that reformulates the norms and subverts the codes. Their cities are a map that questions our own, and their gardens and provinces reshape the natural and cultural order" (30).

labyrinth is on display in Borges's "El jardín de los senderos que se bifurcan," a story in which the protagonist, a Chinese man working as a spy for the German Reich, comes across a labyrinthine garden designed by his great-grandfather. This story contrasts the belief of a Chinese ancestor—a belief that holds that time is not uniform and absolute—with those of Schopenhauer and Newton, a Western philosopher and scientist/mathematician, respectively. This garden of forking paths is an infinite place where the forks are divergences in time rather than in space: "*Crea*, así, diversos porvenires, diversos tiempos, que también proliferan y se bifurcan" ("El jardín" 107). Interestingly, the garden was designed in concert with an infinite, circular novel whose solution to the apparent contradictions is also bifurcations in time. This "red creciente y vertiginosa de tiempos divergentes, convergentes y paralelos" (109) allows for people to exist or not exist in separate timelines.

In *Verde Shanghai*, Cristina Rivera Garza masterfully navigates the blurry waters of a reality described and utilized by Borges: labyrinthine, infinite, circular. The author purposefully leaves ambiguous many passages of the novel. The readers are not restrained to any solution to the Marina/Xian question provided by the characters themselves in their own realities; therefore, the readers can imagine possibilities that lead to separate realities, leading them to a circular, infinite story.

"El olvido es una boa que se muerde la cola. Toda mordida es un círculo" (*Verde* 17). This relationship between a circle and oblivion defines the structure of *Verde Shanghai*. As Marina tries to recuperate her lost memories and past, the novel's structure reflects not a linear temporality, but rather one that circles, looping back into the past to recover a memory and then advancing forward again into Marina's present. Opening the doors to a new reality, this cycle of oblivion and memory for Marina intersects in the past with a separate timeline for Xian.

In one of the first recovered memories, Marina is "baptized" with the name Xian[44] by a woman in a flowered skirt who seems to know her and invites her to have a drink at a bar where the bartender is named Mauricio (25-28). Separately, in Xian's present, Xian finds herself in a bar and also meets a woman in a flowered skirt. Xian introduces herself and they are given drinks by a bartender named Mauricio. While Xian experiences déjà-vu, her companion seems aware of yet unaffected by the strange, repeating temporality. "—¿Ya habías estado aquí, verdad?—la mujer hacía como que preguntaba pero en realidad lo afirmaba" (233). The posited reality here is one where one person's (Xian's) present can have an impact on another person's (Marina's) past.

In *Verde Shanghai*, time seems to be circular. Memory and oblivion are circular. Even another solution to the very existence of Xian and Marina—that they are mutually dreaming or inventing the other—implies a circle. Although the search for a beginning is natural, as Chiang Wei reminds Marina, the beginnings of stories are difficult, "el mismo problema de siempre" (171). A circle has no beginning; neither does it have an end. Every point of a circle is dependent on the others.

In this idea of circularity as well as Xian's idea of a memory creating its own life, a physical body from legs to face, we are again reminded of Borges. Beyond the Orient being a metaphor for utopia and infinite time, Kushigian states that Borges also used the Orient as a metaphor for memory (23). In his short story, "Las ruinas circulares," a magician creates another being from a dream, painstakingly visualizing each part of the body until it comes into being. Later, however, in

---

44 Baptism, a Christian ritual that indicates spiritual rebirth, was a practice that the Spanish missionaries employed feverishly, sometimes in mass ceremonies, on the natives upon the arrival of the *conquistadores* in the Americas (Chasteen 56). The natives then would receive a new, Christian name. A notable example of this practice is the interpreter and mistress for the conquistador Hernán Cortés, given to him in 1519 as a slave and baptized as doña Marina (Karttunen 292). In *Verde Shanghai,* the reversal of the Occident and the Orient baptism is significant. Marina loses her Christian name and receives a new, Chinese name which makes her smile with the pleasure of being someone unknown: a person without a past. The name Xian, however, is not the key to a new life for Marina, but rather a code for discovering her history.

the circular ruins of a temple, the magician realizes that he must also exist because of a dream of another, which implies a perpetual chain of dreams and dreamers, creations and creators. With Borges as an example, it's no wonder that Marina can conceive of the human body as a fiction.

Although both of these stories by Borges come to an end in words, the created realities stretch on and on beyond the page and into the past and the future. Similarly, *Verde Shanghai* doesn't end when Horacio kidnaps Marina to bring her home. In the final page as Marina is alone in a room the lines of identity again blur:

> Uno nunca sabe qué sucede después.
> Oyó los pasos.
> Supuso que diría: Cristina, tengo algo que contarte.
> O algo parecido. Palabras como ésas. (315)

In these closing lines, the autor seemingly inserts herself into the novel, implying, just like Borges in "Las ruinas circulars," a chain of creators. At the same time, she allows the novel to continue, like the novel in "El jardín," initiating a story that just might circle back to the beginning of *Verde Shanghai* itself.

As Marina leaves her dull and normal existence as a housewife to submerge herself in an oriental world, she is presented with a chance to have her own voice and write her own story. She leaves behind the reality of her dull, normal life and as she is searching for Xian and writing and exchanging stories with Chiang—both her oriental Others—doors are opened to new realities that offer many possibilities for Marina's own identity. While Marina's relationships, identity, and the plot and structure of the novel itself become increasingly complex in the barrio chino, the generally accepted reality cannot function. Therefore, in a space considered to be marginal, a space for the meeting of cultures, Cristina Rivera Garza postulates a new reality, one in which the lines between the Orient and the Occident—self and the Other—are blurred, and in which creation of another is a power not limited to an omniscient and omnipotent god alone. In this space created by the author, the reader is left with the burden or pleasure of deciding what are the answers to *Verde Shanghai*'s questions.

Bibliography

Borges, Jorge Luis. "El jardín de los senderos que se bifurcan." *Ficciones*. Buenos Aires: Emecé Editores. 1959. 97-111. Print.

—. "La postulación de la realidad." *Discusión*. Buenos Aires: Emecé Editores, 1964. 67-74. Print.

—. "Las ruinas circulares." *Ficciones*. Buenos Aires: Emecé Editores. 1959. 59-66. Print.

Butler, Judith. *Gender Trouble: Feminism and the Subversion of Identity.* 2nd ed. New York: Routledge, 2006. Print.

Chasteen, John Charles. *Born in Blood and Fire.* New York: W.W. Norton & Company, 2001. Print.

Estrada, Oswaldo. "Cristina Rivera Garza, en-clave de transgression." *Cristina Rivera Garza: Ningún crítico cuenta esto....* Ed. Oswaldo Estrada. Chapel Hill: The University of North Carolina at Chapel Hill, 2005. 27-46. Print.

Fernández Ferrer, Antonio. *Ficciones de Borges: En las galerías del laberinto.* Madrid: Cátedra, 2009. Print.

Gies, Martha. "Old México." *The Women´s Review of Books* 21.1 (2003): 11-12. *JSTOR.* Web. 3 Mar. 2012.

Giordano, Enrique A. "El juego de la creación en Borges." *Hispanic Review.* 52.3 (1984): 343-366. *JSTOR.* Web. 3 May 2012.

Hind, Emily and Cristina Rivera Garza. "Entrevista con Cristina Rivera Garza." *Entrevistas con quince autoras mexicanas.* Ed. Emily Hind. Madrid: Iberoamericana Vervuert, 2003. 185-198. Print.

Karttunen, Francis. "Rethinking Malinche." *Indian Women of Early Mexico.* Ed. Susan Schroeder et al. Norman, OK: University of Oklahoma Press, 1997. 291-312. Print.

Kristeva, Julia. "Word, Dialogue and Novel." Trans. Seán Hand. *The Kristeva Reader.* Ed. TorilMoi. New York: Columbia University Press, 1986. 34-61. Print.

Kushigian, Julia. *Orientalism in the Hispanic Literary Tradition: In Dialogue with Borges, Paz, and Sarduy*. Albuquerque: University of New Mexico Press, 1991. Print.

Lemus, Rafael. "La novela después de la teoría." *Letras Libres*. Editorial Vuelta, Jul. 2011. Web. 19 Jul. 2012.

Molloy, Sylvia. *Signs of Borges*. Trans. Oscar Montero. Durham, NC: Duke University Press, 1994. Print.

Mouffe, Chantal. "Por una política de la identidad nómada." *Debate feminista* 14. 7(1996): 3-12. Web. 21 Mar. 2012.

Ochs, Elinor and Lisa Capps. "Narrating the Self." *Annual Review of Anthropology* 25 (1996): 19-43. Web. 21 Mar. 2012.

Ortega, Julio. *Poetics of Change*. Trans. Galen D. Greaser. Austin: University of Texas Press, 1984. Print.

Rivera Garza, Cristina. "Saber demasiado." *Cristina Rivera Garza: Ningún crítico cuenta esto....* Ed. Oswaldo Estrada. Chapel Hill: The University of North Carolina at Chapel Hill, 2005. 17-19. Print.

—. *Verde Shanghai*. México: Editores Tusquets, 2011. Print.

Said, Edward W. *Orientalism*. New York: Vintage-Random House, 1979. Print.

Samuelson, Cheyla. "'Algo destrozado sobre la calle': *La guerra no importa* como obra precursora en la narrativa de Cristina Rivera Garza." *Cristina Rivera Garza: Ningún crítico cuenta esto....* Ed. Oswaldo Estrada. Chapel Hill: The University of North Carolina at Chapel Hill, 2005. 49-72. Print.

Samuelson, Cheyla Rose and Cristina Rivera Garza. "Writing at Escape Velocity: An interview with Cristina Rivera Garza." *Confluencia* 23.1 (2007): 135-145. *JSTOR*. Web. 3 Mar. 2012.

Soud, Stephen E. "Borges the Golem-Maker: Intimations of 'Presence' in 'The Circular Ruins.'" *MLN* 110.4 (1995): 739-754. *JSTOR*. Web. 3 May 2012.

Tinajero, Araceli. *Orientalismo en el modernismo hispanoamericano*. West Lafayette, IN: Purdue University Press, 2004. Print.

ABOUT THE EDITOR

Araceli Tinajero is Professor of Spanish at The Graduate Center and The City College of New York. She is the author of *Orientalismo en el modernismo hispanoamericano; El Lector: A History of the Cigar Factory Reader;* and *Kokoro, una mexicana en Japón.* Tinajero is the editor of *Cultura y letras cubanas en el siglo XXI* and *Exilio y cosmopolitismo en el arte y la literatura hispánica.* She has co-edited two volumes: *Technology and Culture in Twentieth Century México* (with J. Brian Freeman) and *Handbook on Cuban History, Literature, and the Arts: New Perspectives on Historical and Contemporary Social Change* (with Mauricio Font).Tinajero is the founder of *The City Reading Club* and the co-founder of the Mexico Study Group at the Bildner Center for Western Hemisphere Studies. She is the Book Review Editor of *TRANSMODERNITY: Journal of Peripheral Cultural Production of the Luso-Hispanic World:* http://escholarship.org/uc/ssha_transmodernity

Index

www.ingramcontent.com/pod-product-compliance
Lightning Source LLC
Chambersburg PA
CBHW021236090426
42740CB00006B/553